THE
DIALOGUES
A Meditation on the Gender of Christ

D. Keith Mano

THE FERGUS DIALOGUES

A Meditation on the Gender of Christ

D. Keith Mano

International Scholars Publications
San Francisco - London - Bethesda
1999

Library of Congress Cataloging-in-Publication Data

Mano, D. Keith.
    The Fergus dialogues : a meditation on the gender of Christ / D.
    Keith Mano.
        p. cm.
    Includes bibliographical references and index.
    ISBN 1-57309-299-1 (alk. paper). -- ISBN 1-57309-298-3 (pbk. :
    alk. paper)
    1. Imaginary conversations. 2. Jesus Christ--Psychology.
    3. Dialogues, American. 4. Gender identity. I. Title.
    PS3563.A56F47   1998
    812'.54--dc21   98-7756
                                                            CIP

Copyright 1998 by D. Keith Mano

Editorial Inquiries:
International Scholars Publications
7831 Woodmont Avenue, #345
Bethesda, MD 20814

To order: (800) 55-PUBLISH

TABLE OF CONTENTS

ACKNOWLEDGMENTS

In July of 1994 I completed a thirty page thesis entitled "Jesus: Man and Woman." This essay, written in over-dense and highly excited prose, was eventually to become the armature on which *The Fergus Dialogues* would hang.

During that summer and autumn I sent a Xerox of "Jesus: Man and Woman" to just about everyone with whom I could claim some personal history. I continued to do so as subsequent versions of my Fergus and Dan act appeared. The response was perceptive, engaging and generous. Over time it would produce useful abridgments and modulations of emphasis in my thinking. I wish here to thank all—whatever their level of agreement or disagreement—who took time from a vast reading obligation and gave me the benefit of their insight. One or two names (it is inevitable) may have been omitted. Those few will receive apologies and a free lunch at the Metro Diner upon application to me.

Elaine Arata, Gerry Bamman, Dr. Robert Barrett, Renée Bergeron, Hallie Black, Dr. Henry Black, Susannah Black, Jeanne Bowen, Rick Brookhiser, Christopher Buckley, William F. Buckley, Jr., Yusef Bulos, Siobhan Byrne, Gwen Calman, Jeffrey Calman, Ed Capano, Marge Capano, Ray Cave, Jean Cecchini, Philip Cecchini, Sally Cheffy, Steve Collins, Penny Corbin, Dorothy Davis, Angela DelGenovese, Dawn Didawick, Dan Duckworth, Olympia Dukakis, Kathy Klein Eddy, Halayne Ehrenberg, Eleanor Elkins, Dr. William Everett, Sarah Ferrell, Juliet Flynt, Tom Fontana, Paul Fuhrman, Wendy Fulton, Diane Gaffney, Jack Gaffney, Mitchell Galin, Jane Gassner, Albert Gaulden, Merle Golz, Richie Golz, Adam Granger, John Green, Dan Greenburg, Marjorie Halgin, Alice Hattenbrun, Dave Hattenbrun, Dr. Ira Hoffman, Barnard Hughes, Cherry Jones, Anita Keal, Dr. Norman Kelman, Peggy Kumble, Steven Kumble, Ruth Langella,

x

Louis Lapham, Owen Laster, David Laundra, Linda Laundra, Christopher Lehmann-Haupt, Cathryn Lester, Betty Liveright, Herman Liveright, Mike Luciano, Carla Lund, Jane Lund, Martine Lund, Nelson Lyon, Steven Maguire, Susan Maguire, Jeff Manchik, Mary Mano, Don Meinshausen, Judith Wilson, Geoffrey Morris, Sue-Anne Morrow, Tom Nahrwold, Christopher Napolitano, Geoffrey Norman, Mary O'Connor, Arsenio Orteza, Joan Pape, Dara Paprock, Susan Pellegrino, Austin Pendleton, Shari Press, Fr. Raphael Raymond, James Redfield, Dr. Robert Reiss, John Rezek, Natalie Robins, Marilyn Rose, Pat Ryan, Jeanne Safer, Dr. Louis Savas, Rt. Rev. John Schneyder, Irene Schneyder, Dwight Schultz, Anna Doumas Sclafani, Robin Shamburg, Paula Shoots, Gintare Sileika, Alarik Skarstrom, Susan Smyly, Richard F. Snow, Fran Spatafora, Beth Stamp, Hank Stamp, Helen Stenborg, Barbette Tweed, Sam Vaughan, Ed Weinberger, Paxton Whitehead, Sean Whitesel, Ron Wieck, Barbara Winslow, Morty Wolkowitz, Eleanor Wood, and, way out of alphabetical order, my right hand person and daughter-in-law, Karen Primm Mano, whose close editing and cheerful alacrity allowed me to dictate *The Fergus Dialogues* at a time when my body was almost wholly insubordinate.

I took four colleagues into my confidence from the start: Richard Baltzell, David Black, Alan Salant and Harold Schechter. Through their fine-mesh sensibilities, intellectual and artistic, I was able to sift the Fergus material. For three years, at any time of day, they were subject to hour-long phone calls about a Garden of Eden that lies in the woman's reproductive tract, about a proposed Theophysical Universe, or about Adam's rib in Genesis and how it might stand for the human sexual chromosome. Patiently, step-by-step, they kept me company, as I tracked the fantastical spoor that Fergus had left behind. And they brought me ideas: Dick from his profound understanding of Christian thought, Alan from his encyclopedic knowledge of the sciences, Harold from his lifelong study of criminal pathology (it was Harold, a week before we went to print, who discovered Caroline Walker Bynum's book, *Jesus as Mother*). And, through David Black, the most comprehensive and brilliant mind of my acquaintance, I was able to draw on a vast social and psychological and spiritual context that gave me both validation and encouragement. And, even where these four could not relate to Fergus's speculations, they made me feel that—if only at the level of metaphor—I had hit on a scheme of things that was both organic and spiritually pleasing and worth the hard pursuit.

My splendid wife, Laurie Kennedy, kept me at least half sane—not an easy thing to do—throughout the long gestation period. It was she who recommended that I use the dialogue form. And, directly from that suggestion, Fergus came into being.

Finally: Thanks to Dr. Robert West and Ginger McNally of International Scholars Publications for giving Fergus a respectable home and a frequency of his own to broadcast on.

PART ONE

JESUS: MAN AND WOMAN

January 20th, 4:48 a.m. Broadway and 115th Street. Temperature 23 degrees F. With wind chill factor, -7 degrees F. Two men.

DAN: Cab! Hey, cab! Stop! I'll report you to the Taxi Commission. Hey! Damn.

FERGUS: Sir, I'm trying to get some soup from Ta-Kome over there. If you—

DAN: Beat it. I don't need a New York hustle right now. I really don't. Cab! Over here! Cab! Yo! Over here! Damn.

FERGUS: With another thirty cents I can get a soup.

DAN: Are you following me, do I have to call a cop?

FERGUS: No, sir, you do not have to call a police officer. I'm not following you.

DAN: Then how come you're here? I ran across Broadway, then you ran across Broadway. Beat it.

FERGUS: Sir, you're the only person out at this hour, sir– that's all. I just--

DAN: Beat it. Please. Don't bug me. I warn you. I'm cold and I'm tired and I haven't got patience enough to play this game.

FERGUS: I can appreciate that, sir. I haven't eaten since this afternoon.

DAN: I'm sure. Look. I'm sick—we're all sick—sick of this judging. Day in and day out. Who's the real beggar? Who's really homeless and who's ripping us off? Who has the best act? How do I know you won't spend it on booze?

FERGUS: You can come with me to Ta-Kome—

DAN: Why don't you get a job? The rest of us work, why don't you? Wouldn't it be better to get a job than stand in the cold wind at 4 a.m.?

FERGUS: Would you hire me, sir? The way I look now?

DAN: Well, that's the point, isn't it? Why do you look that way? Why don't you—? Cab! Cab! Damn. Shot right past. Saw me talking to you and he actually sped up.

FERGUS: Ah, the truth is—

DAN: The truth is, no cab will stop for me while you're around. Now I don't want to be rude, and maybe I have been, but I give to the United Way, it's the best I can do, and I'm asking you one more time to please back off. You're, like they say, in my space.

FERGUS: I will. I will. But just suppose that I have something you need. Something that'll save you time and money. Would that be worth fifty cents to you?

DAN: Fifty cents now? Oh, I see. Before it was thirty cents.

FERGUS: I was begging back then. Now I'm negotiating.

DAN: Is that so?

FERGUS: I have information you need. I've got insider dope. It's lucky for you I'm here.

DAN: Oh, sure—something your broker told you.

FERGUS: No. No. It's more to the point than that. Well, I'll tell you—the cabbies went on strike at 2 a.m. this morning.

DAN: What? That's bull. They had an agreement.

FEGUS: It fell through. Now, if I could—

DAN: Well, how am I gonna get home?

FEGUS: The subway's running.

DAN: Go from here to Coney Island by train? It'll take me three hours this time of night. Where's a pay phone?

FERGUS: Over across Broadway by the Ta-Kome. And if we could settle up—

DAN: What a night. What a god-forsaken night. No wonder they just passed me by. Oh, and now it's starting to sleet. Wonderful. Oh, wonderful.

FERGUS: Sir, I—

DAN: 461-6185. 461-6185. Hi, Bea? Oh, oh...I'm sorry, I didn't think you'd be asleep already...No, no I'm not at home yet... It's four something. Wait. What's happened is this, the cabs are on strike, it's sleeting out and I can't get home... The subway, well, what I had in mind is—say I sleep on the couch? No fuss, no bother... I know we made a deal and I'm honoring it, but this is an emergency, I'm freezing my nodes off... No, Bea, I can't call Diane... No, I can't call Cynthia either... Don't let's start... No, because Cynthia and Diane do not live anywhere near here, and I haven't had a two-year intimate relationship with them, the way I've had with you... Who says? I say. We've been over this before... For Christ's sake it's ten below zero out here, I've... No. No, I can't barge in on Cynthia or Diane because I don't have that kind of relationship... Bea. Honey Bea. No, I'm not patronizing you. I do not talk that way to my cat. Jesus, he's a male cat... Bea, Bea... Bea, I just left your apartment, remember, thirty minutes ago. I can't've become a stranger in that short time. It's just that I'm very cold and ... No, no please don't sing me the feminist national anthem, not now. Committed? Right now I'm committed to frostbite, that's all. That's all I can think of. My nostril hair is like chicken wire... You won't even notice I'm there, just leave me the key under the mat... She does not spoil me. My mother... Bea... Bea... Bea... oh, please do pray for me, that's just what I need right now. No, I'm not being sarcastic about your Christian beliefs. But what happened to the Good Samaritan, remember him? Huh? Give me a break... Oh, great. She hangs up on me, great.

FERGUS: Sir, if we could settle the bill—

DAN: You again? Have you been standing here behind me all this time?

FERGUS: We agreed, if I told you something—

6

DAN: Who agreed? I certainly didn't agree.

FERGUS: Sir, sir, I know you just had some kind of bad news—

DAN: What business is it of yours? Were you eavesdropping?

FERGUS: I may have heard, but I wasn't eavesdropping.

DAN: Oh, that's a cute distinction.

FERGUS: You're cold, sir. Your teeth are chattering. I suggest you warm up for a while. Go into Ta-Kome and get yourself a hot cup of coffee. Maybe a donut— the raspberry cream ones, they're very good. And while you're at it—if you'd be so kind—pick me up a cup of beef barley soup. I do have seventy cents here—

DAN: All right, don't break my heart. Here's a buck, go get it yourself.

FERGUS: If you don't mind—I try not to wear out my welcome. I don't inspire the appetite. It'd be better if you—the waiter doesn't like me—it'd be better if you bought it. I'll hang around out here.

DAN: Okay, okay.

FERGUS: Don't forget the saltines. Get an extra pack if you can. Two packs.

DAN: Okay. Let me get through the door.

FERGUS: Right. I'll be waiting out here.

DAN: Coffee black, two sugars. You got beef barley soup?

WAITER: Yes. Fresh from yesterday.

DAN: Cup to go. Oh, with crackers. And a raspberry cream donut. Mmm. Make it two.

WAITER: Anything else?

DAN: That's it.

WAITER: Cold.

DAN: Yeah. By the way, you see that guy out there? With the torn knitted JETS hat and the missing tooth?

WAITER: Gus.

DAN: You know him? Is he harmless?

WAITER: Except to your ears. He can talk the ears off a plastic Jesus. Also he stinks. He hasn't took that same coat off since July. Why, you buy this for him?

DAN: No, no. Just had a little chat with him is all. I'm surprised they let him panhandle around here, a college campus and all.

WAITER: Well, he got his regulars, give him money. He's a graduate from here, so he say.

DAN: From Columbia? I graduated from Columbia.

WAITER: Yes, but you make a success of yourself. And, anyhow I don't see his diploma, so it could be all in his head. Who knows? $6.95 please.

DAN: Here.

WAITER: Hold on. I open the door. You got that heavy briefcase. Hey. Hey. Hey. Gus, I tell you and I tell you, stay away from my place.

FERGUS: What's going on? I'm not bothering anyone.

DAN: Sssh. Keep walking, Gus—until he goes back inside.

FERGUS: Did you get extra crackers?

DAN: I even got you a raspberry cream thing.

FERGUS: You did? Gee, I appreciate that. And, listen, my name's not Gus. It's Fergus. Fergus Quirk.

DAN: Fergus Quirk.

FERGUS: The Third. What's your name?

DAN: Let's just call me Dan—and right now old Dan can't take this sleet, it's cutting into him like a chain saw. So. Here's your stuff. I'm headed for the subway, not my favorite place at night, but this wind is murder. Ta-ta. It's been real.

FERGUS: Don't walk so fast, hold it.

DAN: See ya. Eat your soup.

FERGUS: Dan. Dan. You been a prince, but just one more thing.

DAN: I've done my share.

FERGUS: I know you have. But I've got no place to spend the night in this freezing mess. Listen, please spring me the price of a subway token. Huh?

DAN: Oh, no. Sorry. Catch the next sucker. I'm going down these stairs, good-bye. No hard feelings, I hope your luck changes for the better, that's the truth, so long.

FERGUS: Dan, I only need eighty cents, that's all. Dan!

DAN: G'bye. G'bye. (*Descends.*)

FERGUS: Damn it. Damn. You got too desperate, Fergus. Too much like a loser. Oh, no. That does it. No. I can't believe this. He forget my crackers. After all that he forgot my crackers. Is it too much to ask? Huh? Huh? Huh? Huh?

DAN: (*Coming back up the stairs.*) Fergus—

FERGUS: You forgot my crackers.

DAN: Never mind that. I've got something better than crackers. Here.

FERGUS: A token? A whole token? Bless your heart. Bless your heart. There's ice in both my shoes.

DAN: Well, come on down. Get out of the sleet. Hurry.

FERGUS: You go first. With my bum leg I've got to be careful on stairs. Especially in the ice.

DAN: I'll wait.

FERGUS: Don't. You might miss your train.

DAN: Actually. Hold on a minute.

FERGUS: What?

DAN: There's a big black kid just around that bend in the staircase. So you go first—he won't bother you.

FERGUS: Who says?

DAN: No mugger's gonna rob a homeless man.

FERGUS: We don't get robbed, we get stomped to death and set on fire.

DAN: Oh, bull—I'll be right behind you. I'm just afraid he'll grab my briefcase and outrun me in this sleet. Go on down.

FERGUS: Mother Macree.

DAN: Right behind you.

FERGUS: I'll bet.

DAN: Little faster... Oh, I say Fergus—is your uncle still commander of the twenty-fourth precinct?

FERGUS: Say what?

DAN: You know, Lieutenant—Uh, Quirk. Police Lieutenant Quirk. What's his first name again? Your uncle.

FERGUS: I don't have an uncle.

DAN: Hurry. Hurry. Through the turnstile. Is he following us?

FERGUS: Don't see.

DAN: This way, the downtown side.

FERGUS: Hey, relax.

DAN: That's easy for you to say. I was mugged on the 86th Street platform just three months ago. Awful experience. Dreamed about it for weeks.

FERGUS: Sorry to hear.

DAN: Young black kid—but big, way taller than me. Six-three he was at least. Pulled an eight inch kitchen knife on me. This was on a staircase and during rush hour to boot. Took my wallet, took my Rolex. Then on top of that, he threw my glasses down the staircase. Yeah, and my shoes. Made me pull them off and threw them after my glasses. 6:30 p.m. it was. Let me tell you, I haven't felt the same about mass transit since. So pardon me if I sound like a wimp, I've earned it. Earned the right to be a little jumpy.

FERGUS: No apologies needed. Soup's good. Wish you'd gotten crackers.

DAN: Well, I brought you a donut.

FERGUS: Right. No, I'm not ungrateful. Just famished. Hunger is quite an experience. Really plays with your mind.

DAN: Ah. Look—I want to be polite about this... Ah. Would you mind buttoning up your overcoat again? Frankly, there's a terrible stench and... and... your private parts seem to be... ah, herniating out of your pants crotch.

FERGUS: No, they aren't. No, they aren't. I've got longjohns on underneath. As for the smell... I don't think buttoning up will make that much difference.

DAN: Well, try.

FERGUS: Hey, no problem. This is a wonderful coat, by the way. Bought it in London's Saville row. Bet it's warmer than yours. It's just I slept in a dumpster two nights ago. Outside an Italian restaurant... That's old mozzarella you smell. It's a little less cold down here, so the bouquet tends to come out.

DAN: Spare me the details.

FERGUS: I'll step back a ways.

DAN: I don't understand—why aren't you in a shelter tonight?

FERGUS: Well, it's like this—you civilians have an exalted idea about the shelter system. Me, I feel about shelters kind of like you feel about the subway.

See this front tooth? I mean, where this front tooth was? Guy in a shelter knocked it out with a Volkswagen dashboard.

DAN: With a what?

FERGUS: Exactly my question when I woke up. They've got metal detectors and this guy sneaks in with an entire dashboard. Guy's crazy, I don't blame him, but I flopped on his cot by mistake, so he cold cocks me with this piece of scrap metal he's trying to sell. Blammo. Broke my nose, too. Unconscious for five, six hours. Woke up in the Beth Israel ER. And my shoes. You've noticed, though you're too polite to mention it, you've noticed that I've got one shoe on and one sneaker on. Go to the shelter, better make sure your shoes don't match—or they'll be gone by morning. One shoe and one sneaker, even a shelter thief won't steal those. They have their standards.

DAN: Sorry I asked.

FERGUS: Out on the street, no matter how bad it is—at least there's a chance for a real score. Meet someone generous like you.

DAN: Please. Don't be sarcastic. I have an ambivalence about the whole begging thing. I've had deaf and dumb guys drop one of their sign language things in my lap—then when I didn't cough up any change, this one "mute" cursed me out in four languages. Frankly, if the waiter at Ta-Kome hadn't said you were a Columbia grad, I'd never have given you that token.

FERGUS: Class of 1962. I have a little clientele here. Some old members of the faculty, like Steve Marcus and James Shenton. They slip me a buck or two when they can.

DAN: I had Marcus and Shenton. I'm class of 1981.

FERGUS: Small world.

DAN: Hey, I got an idea. Why doesn't *Columbia Today* do a cover shoot on you? Big headline. PARENTS. FOR ONLY $25,000 A YEAR YOUR CHILDREN CAN LOOK JUST LIKE THIS MAN.

FERGUS: Mmm. No, let's not do that.

DAN: Sorry. Kinda cruel there. Sorry. Uh—so what was it did you in? Alcohol? Drugs?

FERGUS: Oh, it wasn't as simple as that, my friend. I liked a shot now and then, sure. But it was more the publishing industry and my own cockiness and... and a young wife. The immediate cause, though, was a stroke I had about eighteen months ago. Affected the left side of my brain. That's why I limp and carry my right arm up like this. Also affected long term memory and a few other things.

DAN: That's tough.

FERGUS: Oh, it has its upside. Because I'm essentially left-handed now I think there's more conversation, more equal conversation, between the Yin and Yang parts of my brain. There's more balance between the left side and the right side. Of course, finding oneself broke in a cold town had its impact, too.

DAN: You have no family?

FERGUS: A daughter by my first marriage, she lives in San Diego, But she and her husband are just scraping by.

DAN: And the... the young wife?

FERGUS: She left. With my blessing, I might add. For a while she tried to support us both, but she didn't have the resume' for it. And why should she support us? That wasn't part of the contract. The contract was—oh, that she could go to Elaine's with a respected writer and to pub parties and my editor would give her a contract and I would polish her prose and she would be Tama Janowitz. In return for which I'd get the best sex I ever had—and I'd forget that I was fifty-three years old. And it worked for quite a while. A lot longer than I expected.

DAN: You write? Would I know the titles?

FERGUS: Not unless you're more literate than I think you are.

DAN: Oh. How snippy of us.

FERGUS: No, no. I didn't mean it as an insult. Nobody reads my fiction. Absolutely nobody. But maybe you heard of a non-fiction book I wrote, was a best seller called *The Numbers Racket*. They made it into a movie. *The Numbers Runner*. In 1989.

DAN: Sure. Great performance by—the black actor.

FERGUS: Uh. Yes. Morgan Freeman.

DAN: Yeah. So, you must've got a lot of money for writing that.

FERGUS: I did. And it was the worst thing that ever happened to me. I thought I'd be rich and famous. So I stopped doing magazine work and spent four years and almost all my cash on a big novel. My agent just about croaked. He was right. No one wanted serious fiction. We couldn't sell it. And that was that.

DAN: You spent all your money in four years?

FERGUS: Well, one doesn't like to disappoint a young wife. Nor spoil the image. It was easy really—with the IRS helping out. I had no income. First went the assets, then the home equity loan, then the Keough, then the condo. Then I couldn't pay rent on my one bedroom in Astoria. And here I am. What's your line of work?

DAN: Actor.

FERGUS: You can actually afford to be an actor? In New York? Stage or screen?

DAN: Whichever. I'm working on a one-man show about Ben Franklin. Control your own material, I always say.

FERGUS: Always.

DAN: If you wrote it, they gotta cast you. I always say.

FERGUS: And from Ben Franklin you can make a living wage?

DAN: Oh, no. I do voice-overs. Just did one for Merrill Lynch today. Make around three hundred thousand a year.

FERGUS: But you'd rather do theatre?

DAN: No reason I can't do both.

FERGUS: And Bea?

DAN: Well, I don't know if I should talk about Bea. That's a private matter, don't you think?

FERGUS: Sure. Let's see, she's a feminist and she's P.O.'d because you won't make a commitment after two years, and, worse, you're fooling around with other women, especially Cynthia and Diane. Yes. I guess that's about it. No, she's a Christian, too. She said she'd pray for you, I heard that.

DAN: I don't think we should continue this conversation.

FERGUS: Dan, Dan. Why not? We're just ships passing in the night. Talk to keep the cold away.

DAN: Thanks, but no thanks.

FERGUS: You'll lose her.

DAN: What makes you so sure of that?

FERGUS: Because you've begun to exasperate her. And she's got other things to do. What's her line of work?

DAN: Casting director at an ad agency—voice-overs. That's how we met. She hates her work.

FERGUS: Something else then, women don't just kick guys out—there aren't enough of us to go around as it is. Unless she's got another gig set up. Another guy.

DAN: There's no other guy. Sex isn't a prominent part of her life. In fact, she's studying to be an Episcopal priest.

FERGUS: A-ha. That's it. And you resent this.

DAN: No. Sorry to disappoint you—it's fine with me. Kinky even. I hope she becomes a bishop.

FERGUS: Yes. But sex, you say, isn't a prominent part of her life. And you punish her for that. With Cynthia and Diane.

DAN: Well, she wants me to be committed, she could use a little commitment herself. I go to church with her. I listen to her feminist friends. I support what she wants to do. Is it so much to ask? That she make me feel like a man? Now and then.

FERGUS: D'you love her?

DAN: Here's a picture of her. No, no. I'll hold it.

FERGUS: Wow. Michelle Pfeiffer watch out. Not bad for a guy whose hairline is receding.

DAN: Oh, yeah? Everything's receding on you.

FERGUS: True, true. But you didn't answer my questions. Do you love her?

DAN: Uh-oh. That black kid just came down the stairs. He's looking this way. I knew he was acting kinda fishy up there. He's just laying for some dumb white stiff. I knew it.

FERGUS: Do you love her?

DAN: If she loved me, I'd be asleep and warm on her living room couch—not freezing on the 116th Street subway platform at 5:30 in the morning. A mugger's catch of the day.

FERGUS: Do you love her?

DAN: Yes.

FERGUS: Do you want to win her back?

DAN: I haven't lost her.

16

FERGUS: You'll manage it yet. But, if you do lose her, I know how you can win her back.

DAN: I'm sure. How?

FERGUS: Tell her you've had a vision.

DAN: A vision? Like the Maid of Orleans? I think the Prosac is wearing off, Fergus.

FERGUS: A vision about Jesus Christ. She's going to be a priest, you'll impress her.

DAN: And where do I get this vision?

FERGUS: You buy it from me.

DAN: Ha. I almost got took, you almost caught me leaning the wrong way. Buy a vision? And what's the going price for visions, after you've corrected for inflation?

FERGUS: Depends how much you want to see.

DAN: Coy, aren't we?

FERGUS: But for a teaser and some background. Oh, five bucks.

DAN: Did I actually hear you say, "Five bucks?" If this was 1902 and Einstein himself was standing here with $E=MC^2$ in a secret envelope, even then I wouldn't pony up five dollars. What d'you think—you think I'm from Nebraska or someplace?

FERGUS: Three dollars. With an option to buy more.

DAN: Okay.

FERGUS: Up front. I get the three bucks up front.

DAN: No way. You might just give me a recipe for falafel and walk. Then how do I get my money back? Frisk you for it? Somehow I don't think so.

FERGUS: You earn $300,000 a year and—

DAN: And I intend to keep as much as I can.

FERGUS: Okay. Believe it or not, I do have some dignity. Thanks for the soup. Thanks for the donut, which is my lunch tomorrow. I'm going to take the uptown train to a warm grating I know. G'bye.

DAN: Wait. You're gonna walk past that black thug, duck upstairs and leave me here alone with him?

FERGUS: Like you say, he won't mug me. Hey, how d'you know he isn't a plainclothes transit cop?

DAN: Okay. I get the drift. A protection racket. Here's the three dollars.

FERGUS: Five dollars.

DAN: No, you don't. No, you don't.

FERGUS: Yes, I do. Yes, I do.

DAN: Hold on. Be reasonable. At least give me some idea what we're talking about. What it has to do with Bea.

FERGUS: Tell her you had a vision about Jesus. Tell her you saw that Jesus died in both genders equally on the cross.

DAN: Come again?

FERGUS: That Jesus died as perfect God, which the church acknowledges. That Jesus died as perfect man, which the church also acknowledges. And that Jesus simultaneously died as perfect women, which the church has not yet been informed of. Or, to be more precise, which the church has forgotten.

DAN: Uh-huh.

FERGUS: Well?

DAN: So how does it work?

FERGUS: That's what you pay the five bucks for, to find out.

DAN: Hmmm. I must say it does have a politically correct sound to it. Very PC. Bea tends to like PC things. It would make me seem more compassionate and committed. Wouldn't it?

FERGUS: It would. It would. All that and much more for the low, low price of five dollars.

DAN: Okay. You're on. Let me get my wallet.

FERGUS: Oh, thank you, sir. You won't be disappointed.

DAN: No. Can't do it.

FERGUS: Why not? Why?

DAN: There's a train coming finally. You won't have time.

FERGUS: I'll ride along with you.

DAN: But I'm only going to 59th street, then I'll take the D train to Coney. It's way out of your way.

FERGUS: I have no way—that's the advantage of being homeless. I'm as bereft here as I am in Coney Island. I'll come along—haven't been to the beach in years—and we'll do this intellectual transaction. I'll be Scheherazade on the D train, and you'll run up a bill, and I'll give you a receipt so you can declare me as a charitable write-off.

DAN: Nuts. Damn and nuts. Would you believe this?

FERGUS: What?

DAN: It's a work train, I'll never get home at this rate.

FERGUS: Well, look at it from my angle at least. You'll have time to listen now.

DAN: Train's covered with sleet. Just from being outside at 125th street.

FERGUS: You'll have time to listen—

DAN: Must be a blizzard of ice out there. What am I gonna do?

FERGUS: At least you'll have time to listen—

DAN: Oh, please—are you still selling that? Look, I'm in no mood to piss good money away. Not on some cock and bull story of yours, thanks so much.

FERGUS: Wait a minute, hold on now. Pardon my gall, but I think you fairly committed yourself to giving me five dollars. I believe that's the case.

DAN: Never.

FERGUS: Back before the work train came. You got your wallet out. Yes, you did. You were going to give me five dollars for my ideas about Jesus dying in both genders.

DAN: Well, I've changed my mind.

FERGUS: That's not right. It isn't. You were disappointed about the train and now you're taking it out on me.

DAN: There's no law that says I haveta hand you five bucks for some spiel.

FERGUS: We had a verbal agreement.

DAN: No, we didn't.

FERGUS: We did.

DAN: Don't raise your voice.

FERGUS: I'm not.

DAN: I don't have to listen. I can walk away at any time.

FERGUS: I know you can. I'm just trying to get a fair hearing. That's all.

DAN: The best I can do for you is this—you tell me your story and, if I think it has merit, then I'll pay you the five dollars. Only then. I'm not handing you money on spec. Can't do it. It's against my New York nature.

FERGUS: And I can't give you my most important vision for nothing, just like that.

DAN: Take it or leave it.

FERGUS: Hold on. Suppose I give you a smaller vision for free? A sample on the side. If it rings a bell with you—then you advance me five bucks against the rest. Huh? Suppose I prove to you that one of Jesus's miracles actually did occur? How's that?

DAN: Prove?

FERGUS: Using modern science.

DAN: I don't see how you can prove, well, that something occurred or didn't occur two thousand years ago. Miracles are a matter of faith.

FERGUS: Not in this case. In this case the miracle is a matter of fact. Do I have your hand on this?

DAN: No train coming. Oh, all right.

FERGUS: Like pulling teeth. Okay. How do I start? You know Oliver Sacks, the writer?

DAN: Yes. He did that movie *Awakenings.*

FERGUS: Did you read his book *An Anthropologist on Mars*?

DAN: No.

FERGUS: Well, a month or so ago, I'm in the library and I'm skimming through the book and I come to this chapter on blind people—particularly on blind people who have gotten their sight back again.

DAN: Blind from birth?

FERGUS: Some were. Some had been blind for a shorter time—say ten years. In either case, though, they had terrible times adjusting to sight. Terrible. A few of them actually preferred being blind.

DAN: Preferred blindness?

FERGUS: See, look. Your vision has to be trained. It's not enough having your eyesight handed back to you. Because, without training, everything you see is a jumble. A mess. It takes an infant years of practice—staring, staring—before that infant can differentiate between a mobile, a ceiling and its mother's face. For one thing, we're born without depth perception. It all seems flat. Like a painted picture.

DAN: Interesting.

FERGUS: Sacks has this one case history, Virgil I think his name is. Virgil got his vision back after being blind since childhood. He was fifty or so when they performed the eye surgery on him. Wham—suddenly he could see—wham. But what Virgil saw scared the living daylights out of him. Because it was nonsense. Remember, people who suddenly get their sight back have had no practice seeing. It takes years to see. Years. Virgil had absolutely no depth perception. He was afraid he'd trip over his own shadow. A staircase was like an abstract painting— just vertical and horizontal lines. He *knew* they were three dimensional, he could *feel* them with his hands. But he couldn't *see* three dimensions. Are we on the same page?

DAN: Sure.

FERGUS: Okay. But it's not just lack of depth perception. Blind people who get their sight back, well, they can't organize things. Visually. Virgil can see the cat's ear, the cat's tail, the cat's paws, but—try as he might—he can't see the whole cat. Can't put it together. Even when he's holding the cat in his arms. It's terribly frustrating, you can imagine. He can see, but he can't make sense out of what he's seeing.

DAN: How does this relate to Jesus?

FERGUS: Hold on. I'll get there. I'm reading along and at one point Virgil's wife says something like—this is two months after the operation—she says, "Wow, today finally Virgil figured out how a tree is put together. With the branches on top and the trunk on the bottom holding the branches up." And all at once—it was the reference to trees—all at once I connected it with Jesus's miracle at Bethsaida. In St. Mark's Gospel. You know?

DAN: No. It slips my mind. Somehow.

FERGUS: Well, Jesus goes to Bethsaida and they bring a blind man to him. Jesus spits on the blind man's eyes and lays hands on him. Usual scenario. But then Jesus asks the guy if he can see anything. And the guy says—listen, this is great—the guy says, "I see men as trees, walking."

DAN: "Men as trees, walking?" What does that mean?

FERGUS: It's not a poetic image or a piece of whimsy. No. It's a clinical description. The Bethsaida guy, like Virgil, has gotten his eyesight back. But, but, but—but what he is now seeing makes no sense to him. He sees men as walking trees. He's as confused as Virgil was.

DAN: So Jesus didn't really heal him?

FERGUS: Yes, He did. You don't remember? This is a double-barreled miracle. Jesus has healed the eyes, but he hasn't yet healed the brain. That comes next. Jesus then puts his hands on the Bethsaida guy's eyes for a second time. And this time he can see "every man clearly" as St. Mark reports. Now he has depth perception, now he can organize the visual world. He can truly see. The miracle actually took place.

DAN: You mean that St. Mark says it took place.

FERGUS: No, I mean it actually took place. He was blind. Jesus touched him. He suddenly could see. We know this because he describes exactly what a healed blind man would see. "Men as trees, walking." Only an ex-blind man would know that. The disorientation that Virgil felt. Have I got your attention? Hello?

DAN: Uh—

FERGUS: How else would he know that people like Virgil see nothing but jumble and confusion when they get their sight back? How else would he know? Unless he had actually been blind. And was now seeing. There's no way around it.

DAN: Uh.

FERGUS: Buzzzzzz. Time's up. I've proved it—proved that one of Jesus's miracles did, in fact, occur—I want my five buck advance. Buzzzz.

DAN: Sssh. Wait.

FERGUS: Sorry. No way you can slither out of it—the miracle occurred. Five. You owe me five.

DAN: Not so fast. Wait. Someone pretending to be blind—ah.

FERGUS: No, no. Someone just pretending to be blind would've shouted, "I can see, Jesus, I can see." A faker wouldn't know how the world looks to a healed blind man. Only a healed blind man would know that—that men look like "trees walking." Do I have to keep repeating myself? Hey, Dan, are you with us? Yoo-hoo.

DAN: Wait. How can you know for sure? Maybe some doctor back then heard about it from a blind man. That the world's all crazy when you get your sight back. And he tells the phony blind man to pretend—uh—that he sees gibberish. Or maybe someone changed the text later on. And added the part about men who look like trees. It's possible.

FERGUS: Dan. Dan, don't make me weep with frustration. Please. Let me say this just once—you've got no motive. You've got no motive. You've got no motive. Right? St. Marks Gospel—blessed as it may be—St. Mark's Gospel is pro-Jesus propaganda. So are Matthew, Luke and John. Pro-Jesus, wouldn't you say?

DAN: Of course.

FERGUS: Well, but—the Bethsaida miracle, the two-part healing, doesn't make Jesus look good. He's supposed to be the Son of God, why can't he heal this blind man on the first try? It's lousy propaganda. No Christian would've added the "men as trees" part later—or faked it on the spot—because it leaves Jesus looking less than fully competent. As miracle workers go.

DAN: Why is it there, then?

24

FERGUS: Because that's the way it happened. And St. Mark—the oldest and the least flowery of the evangelists, by the way—St. Mark had reverence enough to keep the historical account accurate. Even if he didn't understand the medical significance of the "men as trees" reference. Hell, I didn't know about post-blind syndrome until I read Sacks last month. Did you know about it before now?

DAN: No.

FERGUS: And we live on an off-ramp of the information highway. Dan, Dan, can I please have my money?

DAN: Suppose—

FERGUS: Be a sport—huh?—cough it up.

DAN: Suppose. Well, suppose the man wasn't really blind. I mean, he was really blind—he couldn't see—but there was nothing wrong with his eyes. Say, suppose he had a traumatic shock or hysteria or something. And Jesus healed him by, oh, the power of positive thinking or by His charisma. Laying on of hands stuff. Like you see in the south. It happens, but there are psychological reasons. It isn't a miracle.

FERGUS: Dan. All you do is prove my case for me. Sure—sure there are cases of psychosomatic blindness. Sure. And curing them is no miracle. But that only accounts for part one of the Bethsaida thing. Jesus could maybe uncloud the mind without a miracle. But only by a miracle could Jesus instantly endow that mind with years and years of seeing experience. That's the miracle. Doctors living even now can't do it—they can heal Virgil, operate on Virgil's eyes, no miracle, but they can't teach him to see a staircase or to understand that the cat is a whole animal. Right? Right? It was a miracle at Bethsaida. It happened. *Au revoir. Arrive 'derci.* So long.

DAN: Can you break a twenty?

FERGUS: Are you serious? I can't even break wind.

DAN: It's okay. I've got five singles. Here.

FERGUS: Thanks. Thanks. Hey, give some credit. You got to admit I came up with a pretty elegant proof, huh? Huh? We all could use a little validation. Huh?

DAN: Well, I haven't really given it my full attention. Mostly I've been thinking how cold I am.

FERGUS: Oh, stop withholding. Think what I've done. You prove that one New Testament miracle really happened, then all miracles—all of them—suddenly become possible. Like the meteor from Mars that had signs of life on it. You only need one such meteor and right away life on Mars—anywhere on Mars—life anywhere on Mars becomes possible. Other miracles, walking on water, the Resurrection itself—you have to take them seriously. Not as fairy stories, but as historical, physical events. Hey? Hey, what happened to your coffee?

DAN: Oh, I threw it in the trash can a long time ago. Didn't you see me? It was half empty and cold.

FERGUS: You threw it out? You didn't think to ask me first? Ask if maybe I wanted some?

DAN: It was dredged from the East River to start with. And it was cold.

FERGUS: Did it have real sugar in it?

DAN: Yes.

FERGUS: One or two?

DAN: Two.

FERGUS: Two. That's at least 30 calories you threw away. If I don't have at least 600 calories a day, I start hallucinating.

DAN: Sorry.

FERGUS: Now I'm tempted to eat my donut, damn it all.

DAN: Well, go ahead. Who's stopping you?

FERGUS: I was saving it—I am saving it. To go with a cup of coffee later.

DAN: Give yourself a break. Eat it.

FERGUS: I'm learning to postpone gratification.

DAN: That's silly.

FERGUS: If I were sure I'd have a good meal tomorrow—then maybe I could eat it.

DAN: Well, I gave you five dollars already.

FERGUS: Five. That just pays for part one. The stuff about Jesus and gender. The mystic spear stuff. Not the whole thing.

DAN: How much is the whole thing, dare I ask?

FERGUS: It's $25 if you buy the entire set in advance, up front. Part by part it costs a lot more.

DAN: $25? Have you ever actually been paid $25 for this song and dance?

FERGUS: Yes, since you ask. Three times. And, let me tell you, nobody goes away disappointed.

DAN: Well, we'll see. What time is it anyway? Ten to six. Good grief, we've been down here almost an hour already. And that black kid is still by the stairs.

FERGUS: Relax. There must be a dozen people on the platform now. He's harmless. May I begin?

DAN: Oh, that's all right, you don't have to. Keep the five. The miracle stuff was very provocative. Call it a write off.

FERGUS: But, if I don't tell you about the spear—then I can't sell you the later parts.

DAN: Don't worry about it.

FERGUS: I do worry about it—this is how I make my living.

DAN: It's late. The train will come. You probably won't have time anyway.

FERGUS: I'll talk fast. Let me start.

DAN: Sure. Just take one teeny step back. There. You're a bit, uh, gamy.

FERGUS: Now that you're through humiliating me... where was I? Oh, yes. First, as a preface, I come to all this as a traditional, conservative Christian. And—so it happens—as an Episcopalian, like your lady friend. I don't want to scare people. I keep within the boundaries of accepted Christian theology. Pretty much. Now and then I add a little to the tradition. I do not seek to offend anyone. Pay attention.

DAN: Just looking down the tunnel. I can listen and do that. You don't seek to offend anyone. Go on.

FERGUS: There is a fault line that underlies all Christian churches. A crack in the foundation. Call it gender difference. Call it Yin and Yang. That sort of thing.

DAN: Yin and Yang. Don't go New Age on me, Fergus.

FERGUS: What I'm trying to say is this—women have never been comfortable, never been truly at ease, in the Christian churches. They've felt somehow unclean—almost in the Biblical meaning. Mutilated. Incomplete. Set apart. Weak. Affected by the tides. Certainly subordinate to men. Heck, even in the Episcopal church, which is courteous to a fault—where women can be priests—the air of polite condescension is like thick incense. Women feel it.

DAN: Don't get Bea started on that. Unfortunately, as I tell her, Jesus Christ had testicles. God has always been depicted as a male. I'm not saying it's good or bad, but—

FERGUS: But they have a good argument, women do. Here it is. Jesus—as Christian theologians will tell you—Jesus was incarnated as perfect man. The Word was made flesh. Jesus was made flesh so that He could experience all of our pain and frailness, our humanity. Only by taking on our humanity—fully and absolutely—only then could Jesus make Himself a fitting sacrifice for our sins. The Christian churches have always believed that. It's the cornerstone of their faith. Unfortunately theologians have never followed their thinking to its logical conclusion. Which is?

DAN: You're asking me?

FERGUS: The logical conclusion is: if Jesus was perfectly human and knew all our suffering—if... If so, did Jesus also know menstrual pain and the pain of childbearing?

DAN: Ah.

FERGUS: If He didn't know those things, then He wasn't fully human, His sacrifice was incomplete and we are not saved. Period. Either that or women are inferior and the Gospel should say, "And the Word was made man-flesh only." But the Christian churches have never dared say that—that women were flat-out inferior. Jesus, after all, was born of a very special woman. On the other hand, churches have never wanted to give women equal standing—because women could then lay claim to the priesthood.

DAN: So you favor having female priests?

FERGUS: Oh, it's not really so important. It's a false issue really. The pivotal question isn't whether women should be priests or not. The real question is whether there should be priests in the Christian churches at all. There is a cathedral, I think, inside every believing Christian. If women have to be priests before we can understand that... well, so be it.

DAN: Hmmm.

FERGUS: But if Jesus died in both genders equally—well, then there is no problem. Men and women are equal in Him. It's a mystical teaching of the church.

DAN: Where does the church teach that?

FERGUS: In St. John. At the crucifixion. That's one place. St. John wrote: "But when they came to Jesus, and saw that He was dead already, they brake not His legs: But one of the soldiers with a spear pierced His side and forthwith came there out blood and water." Blood and water. The spear doesn't appear in Matthew, Mark and Luke. The blood and water are not mentioned in Matthew, Mark and Luke. Only in St. John do these things appear. In a gospel written long after Jesus died. Long after the other three gospels were written. Strange isn't it?

DAN: Are you implying that it didn't really happen?

FERGUS: It could have. St. John could've been an eye-witness to it, a very old eye witness—but, look, it doesn't matter whether we're dealing with a historical event or with a powerful symbol. Either way, that spear has become central to the Christian story.

DAN: How so?

FERGUS: It's an all-purpose tool. Like a Swiss Army knife. Look what it does, symbolically at least. First of all, the spear penetrated Jesus as no nail could. The nails went *through* Jesus's body—the spear *implanted* itself. I think we can note a phallic shape there, a phallic action there, without obsessing on it. In conventional Christian art Jesus's spear wound resembles a female's sexual point of entry. Jesus, furthermore, was pierced by a well-meaning male. That Roman soldier who wanted to keep Jesus's body from having its legs broken. It was an act of love, the piercing was.

DAN: I catch on. The soldiers—

FERGUS: Let me finish. St. John says, "And forthwith came there out blood and water." What's this business about blood and water? Those two symbolic liquids don't appear side by side anywhere else in the New Testament. It's an extraordinary moment in the Passion. St. John is very insistent about it. "And he that saw it bare record, and his record is true: and he knoweth that he saith true, that ye might believe." Yet the Christian churches have been very quiet about it. We don't say, "Drink ye all of it, for this is my blood and water of the New Testament." We conveniently forget the water, don't we?

DAN: So you're saying—

FERGUS: Well, when do human beings expel water from their bodies?

DAN: Uh. Oh. Breaking water. Women do. Just before they give birth.

FERGUS: Aha. Took you long enough. The birth sac breaks. So St. John—in a mystical reference to Jesus's female nature—St. John is indicating to all Christian women that the Savior, like so many females of the biblical era, died in childbirth.

DAN: Jesus died in childbirth. But what was the baby?

FERGUS: On the cross Jesus gave birth to a new dispensation. To Christianity. To the Church. To a hope of salvation. In fact the spear, the blood and the water provide a compound image for the entire procreative process. From penetration to the birth of an infant by C-section.

DAN: Not bad. Jesus died in childbirth. Bea would love to hear that.

FERGUS: But that's not all. The spear—as it is depicted in European art—acts the way an anatomist's pointer would. It's been trying to get our attention for almost two thousand years.

DAN: Attention to what?

FERGUS: Well, St. John wrote that the spear "pierced His side." What do you consider your side?

DAN: About here.

FERGUS: Right. Somewhere below the belly and above the abdomen. When I get a stitch in my side that's where I feel the pain. And yet traditional Christian art places Jesus's side in a very different area. Up here. Under the lowermost rib, left or right. At just the rib most conveniently removed by God—so that Eve could be made.

DAN: Eve? Where did she come from?

FERGUS: From Adam's rib. Jesus is referred to by the Church as Second Adam. The spear thrust, understood mystically, heals the wound in First Adam's side. Where Adam's rib was removed so that Eve could be created. At the crucifixion our sexual difference is repaired. Because, in Jesus, both genders are equally present. Adam and Eve are one.

DAN: I think I get it. The spear in Jesus's side... uh. It—am I right?—it restores...

FERGUS: St. John was signaling to Christian women. "Look," he was saying, "Look, Jesus is fertile just like you. Jesus is vulnerable and submissive just like you. Jesus feels your agony. And, in His sacrifice, the sad events of the Creation are made whole."

DAN: The first part I get. The second part about the Creation—I could use some remedial work there.

FERGUS: For that we have to re-enter the Garden of Eden.

DAN: So. Let's. What is it?

FERGUS: A train's coming.

DAN: You can't be serious. Finally. So that's what a train looks like.

FERGUS: Warmth. Warmth. Warmth.

DAN: What were you saying about the Garden?

FERGUS: There's another payment due. I can't go into the Garden without another payment.

DAN: How much?

FERGUS: Ten dollars.

DAN: That's absurd.

FERGUS: No, it's not absurd. This is a major mystery I'm revealing here. It's time I got a decent commitment from you. That's not too much to ask. Ahhh. Finally some warmth. Step in.

P.A. SPEAKER: Next stop 110th Street.

FERGUS: Warmth, warmth, warmth.

DAN: I think that black kid got on.

FERGUS: Shiver when I thaw out. I d-d-don't shiver when I'm cold. Keeping my b-b-body stiff against the wind—uh, uh, uh—it sort of locks on m-muh. Me. Sit down.

DAN: Just keeping an eye on the next car.

P.A. SPEAKER: This is 110th and Cathedral Parkway. 103rd Street next.

DAN: Where do you think the conductor is? Two cars back?

FERGUS: Dunno. Relax. Are we changing to the D at 59th Street?

DAN: Yuh.

FERGUS: Why's a b-b-big money guy like you…live, uh, in a God forsaken dump like Coney?

DAN: It's not so bad. I only go into the city two-three times a week. Besides it's free.

FERGUS: Free?

DAN: My mom and dad bought a condo—so, when Dad died three years ago, there was this extra room. Mom doesn't get lonely. I don't have to pay rent. It's good. I kick in for the food. It works out.

FERGUS: You still live with your mother?

DAN: Want to make something of it?

FERGUS: No, no. Bea must love that—you living with your mother.

DAN: She likes it fine.

FERGUS: Uh-huh.

P.A. SPEAKER: 103rd Street. Next stop 96th Street.

DAN: Look, ten dollars, I think it's too much.

FERGUS: D'you feel cheated so far?

DAN: No. Not really. I mean—no. But—call me paranoid—maybe it's my New York cynicism—I don't know. I just have this horror of getting ripped off. Its not the money per se. I mean, what do I tell my friends—I paid ten dollars to some homeless man on the subway so he'd give me a talk about the Garden of Eden? "Oh, yeah?" my friends would say, "And do I *ever* have a bridge to sell you."

FERGUS: Why, tell me why, why you have to mention this conversation at all? To anybody?

DAN: I don't, I don't. It's just. Well. If you'd give me some idea what we're talking about—

FERGUS: A movie trailer, a jacket blurb?

DAN: Well. Something like that.

FERGUS: Y'know, pardon me for saying this, but... I mean, I could get pretty ticked off... I am ticked off. For an hour I've been entertaining you. Hell, you didn't have much else to do. Apparently there's no book in that briefcase of yours to read—

DAN: Wait up. I paid you five dollars, plus the food. That's pretty good for an hour's work. Tax free.

FERGUS: Oh, how magnificent of you. How splendid. Tell me—what would you spend on flowers, making up with your girlfriend? Forty dollars at least. At least. Here I am, like Cyrano de Bergerac, giving you lines so you can woo Roxanne. Plus I'm offering to travel with you all the way to Coney Island. Hey, the laborer's worthy of his hire. Ideas are all I've got to sell, and, dang it, I'm not giving them away for nothing.

P.A. SPEAKER: 96th Street, express across the platform. 86th Street next.

FERGUS: Mind now, I'm grateful for what you've done. It's not often I get a chance like this—to talk with a tax-paying citizen. And a Columbia grad as well. Not to mention the donut.

DAN: No problem. No problem. I apologize if I—you're obviously an intelligent man. Obviously.

FERGUS: But no ten bucks?

DAN: Y'gotta give me something to go on. It's my nature.

FERGUS: I see, you have to be in control of everything, eh?

DAN: Maybe. Whatever.

FERGUS: Okay, then. This is my best offer. I give you a teaser. One sentence. If that one sentence is intriguing enough, you pay me twenty dollars, and—

DAN: Twenty—?

FERGUS: Don't go into cardiac arrest on me. Listen. Listen. Twenty bucks for the whole thing. It's fifteen percent off my wholesale price. For twenty bucks you get the entire vision. Everything. That includes the Garden of Eden, the Mystery of Differentness, the Nature of God and—as they say—much, much more.

DAN: Twenty—?

FERGUS: Dan—I can't keep stopping and starting. It destroys my narrative flow. And it insults me—that somehow I haven't earned your trust yet.

P.A. SPEAKER: 86th Street. 79th Street will be next.

FERGUS: Well?

DAN: All right, give me the teaser.

FERGUS: Twenty or nothing now. Up front.

DAN: Yes. Go ahead.

FERGUS: Hmmm. A sound bite is what you want. Okay. Here it is. The Garden of Eden lies in every woman's reproductive system.

DAN: Huh?

FERGUS: The Garden of Eden lies in every woman's reproductive system.

DAN: I heard you. But how in the reproductive system? You mean in the womb?

FERGUS: Dan. That's what you pay to find out. But no. Not in the womb. More than that I won't say.

DAN: I've got to think a minute.

FERGUS: You do that. We got seven minutes to 59th Street. And in the meanwhile I'll doze a bit. Wake me up if you find a twenty dollar bill. Otherwise I'll stay on the train where it's warm.

P.A. SPEAKER: 79th Street, watch the doors. Next stop 72nd Street, change for the express Number Three. This is 72nd Street. Next stop 66th Street, Lincoln Center. Stand clear of the doors, please. 66th Street. Next stop 59th, change for the A, B, C and D trains. This is 59th Street, Columbus Circle.

DAN: Fergus. We get off here.

FERGUS: Where are we?

DAN: Columbus Circle. Get up.

FERGUS: It's warm here. You buying?

DAN: Yes. Yes, hurry. I'm buying.

FERGUS: Not so fast. My foot's asleep. Ow.

DAN: I don't want to miss the D if it's coming.

FERGUS: Dreamer. You go ahead. I can't rush like this on the staircase, I've got pins and needles.

DAN: Hurry.

FERGUS: See, I told you. There's no train.

DAN: It must just have come and gone—there's nobody on the platform.

P.A. SPEAKER: Due to fizerks sum tamblin, D trains wooby nafta sum gawl. Scrawk!

DAN: What language is that?

P.A. SPEAKER: Due to fizerks sum tamblin, D trains wooby nafta sum gawl.

FERGUS: I'm glad he repeated it. I wasn't sure what I heard the first time.

DAN: Didn't sound good.

FERGUS: Well, I need time to explain how Jesus is man and woman. Complete man and woman. Got my money?

DAN: Here. Don't tell anyone I did this.

FERGUS: Your secret is safe with me. Now. Let's see. Oh, yes. I forgot. I have to brainwash you first. When I speak about the two halves that make a perfect whole—well, often I'll say "male" and "female." It's a habit we get into. You hear me say that—you hear me say male and female—I want you to say in your head, "Fergus doesn't mean that, he means something closer to Yin and Yang. Or the vanilla and the fudge in vanilla-fudge ice cream." Anything to get away from that reflex image we have of a naked woman and a naked man. Don't limit it to sex and gender.

DAN: Sst. The black kid's here. He's sitting on the top stair behind you. Can just see his sneakers.

FERGUS: That's not him, that's another black kid.

DAN: It's him.

FERGUS: What did I just say?

DAN: That "male" and "female" are limiting stereotypes. You want to use more general terms when you indicate the opposite halves that make a whole.

FERGUS: Not opposites. Not opposites. Complementary parts that make up a whole. Blue and red aren't opposites. Together they make a whole that we call purple. Which is entirely different from either blue or red.

DAN: Yup. Move so I can watch him over your shoulder.

FERGUS: Dan, may I presume that you know the Garden of Eden story from the Book of Genesis?

DAN: You may.

FERGUS: Dan, I'm going to ask that you take a leap of imagination with me. A leap that'll change your view of God and Creation both. So. What, tell me, is the Adam and Eve story about?

DAN: First of all it's a myth, not a story. And it's about the creation of our species.

FERGUS: Right—that's the standard answer. Nothing wrong with it. Except I believe there's a more important and edifying interpretation. One that nobody in five thousand years has ever stumbled over.

DAN: And you're dying to tell me.

FERGUS: Dan, I think the Adam and Eve myth isn't just about the species. No. It's also about our own personal and *biological* creation. Your creation. My creation. Your girlfriend's creation. The Adam and Eve myth is about sexual reproduction.

DAN: How so?

FERGUS: The Garden of Eden lies in the female egg. In all female eggs before they're fertilized.

DAN: Yeah, that. I want to hear more about that.

FERGUS: Cup your hands.

DAN: Like so?

FERGUS: Right. Now imagine that's the egg of a human female. Your mother's egg maybe. Each month one egg developed from one follicle in your mother's ovary. In that egg—cup your hands—in that egg there is all the potential for a complete male child or a complete female child. Both Adam and Eve are in that egg.

DAN: How both?

FERGUS: Well... What's a simple analogy I can use? Mmm. A Castro convertible sofa. If no one shifts it over, then it'll remain a sofa. But it still has full potential to be a bed. So the egg could produce a male child if it were fertilized to produce a male. Or female if female. In your cupped hands is a mix of chemical and electrical and chromosomal material that together makes a perfect whole. All male and all female. All Yin and all Yang. It's this harmonious, complete place that our Collective Unconscious remembers as the Garden of Eden. Where there was no competition. Where the two genders lived as one in love. In the egg.

DAN: Until Eve went and ate the apple. I tease Bea about that. She says women were framed.

FERGUS: And she's right.

DAN: Is she?

FERGUS: Let's see what you know about The Fall of Man. Genesis mentions two trees—growing right there in your cupped hands. God told Adam and Eve not to eat fruit—traditionally an apple—from one of those two trees. Which one?

DAN: Which one? Can I put my hands down now? Tree of... well, it's the Tree of Life, no?

FERGUS: Everyone gets that wrong. No, not the Tree of Life. God didn't mind us becoming immortal. That was okay—being immortal was—so long as Adam and Eve were innocent. What God didn't want was for Adam and Eve to eat from that other tree, the Tree of the Knowledge of Good and Evil.

DAN: That tree. Oh, sure. Had it on the tip of my tongue.

FERGUS: Okay. You're so smart—what do we need for the Fall? We need Eve, out for a walk on her own. And we also need an apple from the Tree of the Knowledge of Good and Evil. What else do we need?

DAN: A snake?

FERGUS: Correct. But maybe we can combine those last two things. Make a more powerful symbol from the species's unconscious memory. What has a head like an apple and a tail like a snake?

DAN: Me, you're asking? Well, oh. A tadpole?

FERGUS: Dimwit. What looks like a tadpole?

DAN: Uh—I see. I see. Male sperm.

FERGUS: Yes. The serpent in Genesis symbolizes a male sperm. There really is no "Fall of Man." The so-called "Fall" is, in fact, the moment of fertilization. When the sperm is accepted by the egg. Conceive is a resonant word here. Conceive a child. Conceive the knowledge of good and evil. The so-called "Fall" occurs whenever a woman gets pregnant.

DAN: Interesting. But why do you say "so-called?"

FERGUS: Because—and here, for just the once—here I differ somewhat from conventional theology—I can't see how there could be any sin at the so-called "Fall." The sperm and the egg are innocent. They have no free will. They obediently act out God's plan for them. They seek to procreate, that's all.

DAN: No Original Sin?

FERGUS: No, none.

DAN: Well, that's an improvement. I never could understand Original Sin. God makes a big fuss about giving us free will. Then he charges us with sins occurring ten thousand years before we were born. It does nothing for His image as a nice guy.

FERGUS: But you can understand why man—particularly church men—why they invented Original Sin. The moment of conception is a moment of primal trauma, both for the mother and for the new soul that is suddenly called into existence. It's a moment of sadness. Of loss. And, being guilty humans, we tend to blame ourselves. Not God, certainly not our all-good Father. But *someone* must be at fault, someone's sin must have caused all that sorrow.

DAN: Why sorrow?

FERGUS: Well, for one thing, the peaceful egg, the peaceful Garden of Eden, has been broken into. In Genesis the Fall of Man remembers this first moment of loss. Adam and Even will never be whole again. Never be the perfect Yin and Yang, the red and the blue that make purple together. Suddenly Eve has the knowledge of good and evil. For the first time she knows gender. Separateness. Difference. Mortality.

DAN: Because of conception?

FERGUS: The sperm thunders like a meteorite into the Garden, into the egg. It destroys oneness and balance—for the sperm immediately determines gender. A Y-chromosome sperm switches on the male potential in Eden and drives the female out. An X-chromosome sperm switches on the female potential and drives the male out. In either case Adam and Eve, Yin and Yang, blue and red are made separate forever. You might say that the Y-sperm seduces Adam and forces Eve into exile—the Y-sperm is, I think, the mysterious Lilith of the Kabala. And a male child is conceived. Conversely, of course, the X-sperm seduces Eve and forces Adam, the male potential, into exile. And a girl child is conceived. In either case conception is a terrifying event.

DAN: Where is this exile place?

FERGUS: Well, let's deal with a male child's conception. Speaking biologically, chemically, at the moment of conception all that female potential in your mother's egg, the Eve part, was absorbed back into the Garden's DNA material. It remains in you or me like the perfume left behind by a chaste departed love. Lilith may— with her stranger's DNA—she may have seduced Adam, she may have control, but there are strong aspects of Eve dissolved into Adam. Hidden mystically in Adam.

DAN: Where?

FERGUS: Well, no doubt the female potential of the male is imprisoned everywhere within him. In obvious places—like male nipples—and in secret places. The female potential lies hidden in whichever or whatever part of the brain is recessive. Take me. I don't think I'd be having these, uh, visions, if it weren't because the stroke paralyzed the dominant, male side of my brain. There's more communication now between Yin and Yang.

DAN: The male side of your brain is talking to the hidden female side? That's a bit eerie.

FERGUS: I think the recessive brain—in male and female—is where the imagination lies. Where metaphors are made. Where the Collective Unconscious is heard. The dominant side is too literal. Too darn busy trying to read the road markers, you know. And then there's our sex drive.

DAN: What about it?

FERGUS: The dominant side—that's the male side in men, the female in women—the dominant side in men is obsessed with finding a woman who will take the place of his lost female half. So I hung out with young chicks. And you still chase Cynthia and Diane. But the sad thing is—you can't find the captive, latent, female part of your brain in a Columbus Avenue singles bar. You can't find your long lost partner from Eden there either. Though I sometimes think that, at the moment of orgasm—in those few seconds—we re-experience the Adam and Eve egg union, egg wholeness again. That's one reason we prize simultaneous orgasm.

DAN: So that's why I chase tail? I'm looking for Lady Dan?

FERGUS: Aren't you?

DAN: I haven't thought about it, me all done up in drag.

FERGUS: The Eve you lived with in your mother's egg, in her garden—that Eve was precious to you. For all intents and purposes she was you. She was made of the same DNA. What she thought, you thought. What you lacked, she had. And it was yours to use at will. It still might be, if you could learn to access both sides of your brain equally.

DAN: Would I still need Bea?

FERGUS: Sure. This tribe of men still reproduces by sperm and egg. That may not always be so, what with the progress we've made in cloning. But, right now, you need Bea and Bea needs you. You need Bea, but you might not need Cynthia and Diane and all the others. You'd be secure in your female nature—you wouldn't be driven by a love-hate obsession with women who can never heal your sense of inner loss. Never, because—for one thing—those women are too busy looking in the wrong place for their lost inner male.

DAN: Well, its an engaging theory, but you can't prove it.

FERGUS: Here's another question: a question that I've never yet heard any Christian answer with confidence. Or any Jew for that matter. It tells you in Genesis: "And God said, Let us make man in Our image, after Our likeness." What does that mean to you?

DAN: Oh. Mmm. That God is about six foot with astigmatism and a receding hairline. Also He has trouble with relationships. I don't know. You tell me, that's what you're paid for.

FERGUS: It's a tough one. Unless you drop all preconceptions and examine the question scientifically.

DAN: Scientifically.

FERGUS: Scientifically speaking, what does God create us as? All of us. What are we to start with?

DAN: Ah, amino acids, protein...

FERGUS: In what form?

DAN: An egg?

FERGUS: That was hard. An egg. Now, I've never met the Divinity in person. And, no doubt, being God, He can assume all shapes—but… But, speaking as a novelist, I can't think of any form more appropriate for the creator of universes than an egg tending to roundness like a human female's ovum. Full of all potential. The maleness and femaleness absorbed into a harmonious One. There's no better… ah, logo—for our Father Who art.

DAN: God the omelet. Why hasn't anyone else thought of that? Or has someone?

FERGUS: It's only fairly recently that we've had microscopes strong enough to see the human egg. Before that "egg" meant chicken egg. Ovate. Somehow ovate isn't godlike. God tends to the symmetrical. Hey! Hey, look.

DAN: I think, yes. A D train.

FERGUS: How time passes when you're having fun.

P.A. SPEAKER: Next stop Seventh Avenue. Watch the closing doors.

FERGUS: Warmth. Now I'm gonna start shiv-shivering again. Wish. You. H-hadn't thrown ow-out the coffee.

DAN: Uh. It just struck me. Uh. Would you like a slug of bourbon?

FERGUS: Hello. We have a bad connection, I'm hearing strange things. Hello. Hello, Dan. You mind repeating that?

DAN: I was cleaning out my drawer at Bea's. And I found my old flask—plus some other stuff. Here. Let me open my briefcase. Lean back.

FERGUS: Oh, there's the little rascal. Sure and bless him. How full is it?

DAN: Little more than half I think.

FERGUS: Oh, bless him. What's inside?

DAN: Wild Turkey.

FERGUS: The 80 proof or the 100 proof? I only drink the 100 proof.

DAN: Seriously?

FERGUS: Are you kidding? I'd drink sweat drained off a corpse right now.

P.A. SPEAKER: Seventh Avenue.

DAN: Now we have one little problem. You want me to be frank, don't you?

FERGUS: I'm not so sure.

DAN: We've got to get this into you—but without it touches your mouth. There's a sore on your lip.

FERGUS: I can manage.

DAN: No, Fergus, you can't—take my word for. Even your good hand shakes.

FERGUS: Don't worry about germs. Alcohol is antiseptic. They used the chalice even in plague times.

DAN: This isn't a chalice.

FERGUS: Well, you drink first. Whoa—not so much, leave some.

DAN: There's plenty. Hold your head back, I'll pour it in when we hit a stop.

FERGUS: Do it now, there's no one in the car now. It'll look ridiculous if someone sees you doing it.

DAN: I don't want to spill any. Be patient, here it comes.

P.A. SPEAKER: Rockefeller Center. Change for the F and Q trains. Step in, please.

FERGUS: Gaa-blap. Ow.

DAN: What?

FERGUS: Alcohol on the open sore.

DAN: Sorry.

FERGUS: Sorry? Don't be sorry. Blessed be he who gives a shot of hooch to the least of these my children.

DAN: Enough?

FERGUS: No. No. I haven't felt such warmth in my esophagus since I stole a bottle of Nyquil for Christmas dinner.

DAN: Open up. Damn. Should've waited 'til 42nd Street. Spilled some.

FERGUS: Bless you, Dan.

DAN: You better not take any more on an empty stomach. Give you another slug at Coney.

FERGUS: Makes me feel expansive, it does. Been contracting like the incredible shrunken man for month now. I'll be eloquent again.

DAN: God help us. What I'm gonna do, I'm gonna pour a little on your coat. Improve the odor.

FERGUS: No! No! Don't waste it.

DAN: I just saw, there's lettuce in your collar. And some carrot shreds.

FERGUS: Comes with the main course.

DAN: Should I brush—er—it out?

FERGUS: No. What you can help me with is this—I need to take a leak. And at my age you gotta say prayers to your prostate. Worse, cold weather tightens it up. After we leave 42nd Street, if no one gets on, I'm gonna go between cars. But my leg is shaky when the train is moving and my hands'll be preoccupied, so if you could hold me by the coat so I don't fall.

DAN: Ah—

FERGUS: No, you don't want to. Never mind, I'll manage.

DAN: No, no. It's fine. I've got my gloves. Bea says they're washable.

FERGUS: Oh, I'm glad of that.

P.A. SPEAKER: 42nd Street. Change for B, F, Q trains and Number Seven to Main Street Flushing. 34th Street next.

FERGUS: All clear.

DAN: Maybe we should wait. It's just a short run to 34th. Wait until we're between 34th and the next stop.

FERGUS: No, gotta go. The booze defrosted my plumbing.

DAN: Let me grab the door.

FERGUS: Thanks. Oh, dammit—put my longjohns on backward. Hold onto me, I've got some Houdini work to do here.

DAN: Wait, let me get my gloves on.

FERGUS: Can't wait, hold me upright.

DAN: Oh, nuts, nuts, nuts.

FERGUS: Curses. Wouldn't you know.

DAN: What? We're almost at 34th.

FERGUS: It won't let loose. Make tinkling noises. Dang bladder won't let loose.

DAN: Fergus. Be careful. We'll both fall.

FERGUS: Burns. Gaah—oww. Think I picked up an infection.

DAN: Venereal?

FERGUS: I wish, I wish. Don't talk, I've got to concentrate.

DAN: Hurry. I can't keep holding my breath.

FERGUS: Aaahhh.

DAN: Aaahhh.

FERGUS: What? Oh. I'm awful sorry. Sorry. I didn't judge the wind right. I'm so sorry.

DAN: It's...It's okay. These shoes have seen better days anyhow.

FERGUS: No, it's not okay.

DAN: Here we are. Can you stand? I can't leave my briefcase.

P.A. SPEAKER: 34th Street. West 4th Street next. Watch the doors.

FERGUS: Hah.

DAN: What?

FERGUS: For a moment there—just for a moment—you saw yourself in me.

DAN: What?

FERGUS: As I came towards where you were sitting. Just for a second there you saw yourself. You saw Dan—what's your last name?

DAN: Rusher.

FERGUS: For just a moment you knew—you knew that there wasn't all that much separating Dan Rusher and me. Couple decades in age and marketability, that's about it. Then what? Suppose your vocal cords went? Could you live off your capital?

DAN: I'm good with money. I could make it last five-six years. Then, sure, I'd have to get a job-job.

FERGUS: That's what I thought two years ago. I thought, so I'll have to work? Hey, Faulkner worked in a kerosene factory or someplace. So big deal, I'll work. But guess what—my friends said I was overqualified—a polite way of saying, "You're too old." And strangers, strangers wouldn't even hire me as a receptionist because I didn't know computers. Do you know computers?

DAN: A friend is gonna teach me.

FERGUS: Yeah, I had the same friend. Meanwhile I ended up making phone calls for a telephone research company. "Hi, I'm Fergus, from American Consensus Surveys—may I ask how often per week you use an anti-fungal compound on a) your feet, on b) your head and on c) your private parts? Sorry you feel that way, sir. Have a pleasant evening." Made six bucks an hour, $157 a week take home. And I got fired for not being aggressive enough.

DAN: You were living alone then?

FERGUS: Val, my lady friend, left me about that time. It was a relief. At least then I could pull the blinds down and just feel sorry for myself. I don't blame Val. Our genders had switched. She was the provider, and I was becoming the female in our relationship. Which is cool, as they say—if the other party is also into it, which she definitely wasn't.

DAN: Bea murders me at tennis. Hey—

FERGUS: We've stopped.

P.A. SPEAKER: There is a train halted in front of us. We should be moving shortly. Thanks for your patience.

DAN: New York, New York.

FERGUS: While we've stopped—don't suppose... could I have another shot of booze?

DAN: Why not? I could use one, too. Hmmm, what else have I got here? How about this pair of socks I left at Bea's? They're clean. Here.

FERGUS: Well, thanks, I will. Clean socks are a very special pleasure. What's that red thing in your briefcase?

DAN: Oh, my cummerbund. Bea and I had a formal occasion to attend.

FERGUS: Guess I couldn't wear it?

DAN: A homeless man wearing a cummerbund? I dunno.

FERGUS: A bit pretentious, eh? A bit above my station?

DAN: Well, I don't say that. More like it doesn't go with your ensemble.

FERGUS: Yes, I see that. Still, in New York they expect a little panache. The homeless competition is fierce. There's always someone with a better act. Women with children, they've got a lock on the big money. And the damn violinists. I'm thinking I'll get myself a small dog. A small woeful dog.

DAN: Open up.

FERGUS: Good, good.

DAN: *Skoal*—hey.

FERGUS: Wha?

DAN: Down the other end of the car. I saw a black face in the window. The door window.

FERGUS: Nothing there now.

DAN: Dunno how long he was watching us. But I'm sure it's the same guy. He's waiting for us to split up. Then he'll mug the straggler.

FERGUS: Can't be sure.

DAN: I'm sure. Sure enough. I'm not going through that horror again. Tell me, Fergus—you who know everything except how to get a job—why does God create evil in the world?

FERGUS: He doesn't create evil—He only creates Differentness.

DAN: What's that?

FERGUS: Listen carefully. We're dealing with mysteries here. If anything I say escapes you—well, then stop me. I'll go back over it again.

DAN: Don't be so patronizing.

FERGUS: Fine. So first I've got to explain how Differentness works. It's an essential concept. You gotta get comfortable with it. Differentness. It's a clumsy word, I know, but it gets the point across. See, it's like this. Beyond God's perfect good and the very imperfect good of man—well, there's a vast category of things that are neither bad nor good. They're simply different from one another, understand?

DAN: Keep going.

50

FERGUS: So. A chair is different from a table. A bat from a cat from a hat. Yet if I choose one instead of the other, I haven't committed a moral act. The chair isn't morally better than the table. They're neutral. As are 99 percent of the things we see and do in life. Yet Christians, when they talk of free will, talk as if they were full-time umpires of good and evil. When actually, most often, free will is about whether we go to the drug store or the dry cleaners first thing in the morning. You with me?

DAN: Yes, yes—I'm with you.

FERGUS: I emphasize Differentness. Probably you think I overemphasize it. But, take my word on this, you can't understand the universe and man's history without Differentness. So hold it in the back of your mind.

P.A. SPEAKER: The train ahead of us is moving. We should get a clear signal soon.

FERGUS: Now. I take it for granted that we're speaking about the Christian God here. So, even if you're a Buddhist or an atheist, grant me my first principles. Yes?

DAN: Yes. I'm not an atheist, by the way.

FERGUS: Good. Now what do we know about God? His essentials. Qualities that we can all agree on—Catholic or Unitarian or Baptist.

DAN: Are you asking me?

FERGUS: Well, I thought you might want to participate.

DAN: You're doing just fine.

FERGUS: Okay. Okay. Would you agree that God is good?

DAN: Let me think what Bea would say. Yes.

FERGUS: And would you grant Him all those omni-adjectives—omnipotent, omnipresent, et cetera?

DAN: Okay.

FERGUS: It's a cliché, perhaps. More often said than understood or felt. But let me postulate that God is love.

DAN: Mmm. Bea would go along with that.

FERGUS: Good. We've got something to work with. So. Would you say that Divine Love seeks to do good?

DAN: Move along, I don't need a catheter in my brain, I'm following you.

FERGUS: Good. So God, wherever there is need, seeks to forgive, heal, comfort, absolve. Love, after all, is a transitive verb. It must act upon something. Love that doesn't seek to express itself in action is not love. So maybe we've uncovered a kind of divine physics here. God is not only love. God is also love in motion.

DAN: All right.

FERGUS: So God must have at least one intelligent being to act upon and to love. Healing, forgiving, comforting can only be expressed by intelligent beings as they relate to each other.

DAN: So what you're saying is—

FERGUS: That God must create at least one being different from Himself. At least one intelligent being.

DAN: Must?

FERGUS: Well, think for yourself. If God is alone in the universe and God must love—then we've got Him loving Himself. Which is self-directed, prideful love. Which is narcissism. And a narcissistic God can't be all good. Furthermore there would be no motion involved. God would be sitting in an egg-shaped lump of perfection admiring Himself.

DAN: But if you say God needs something, then you're putting limitations on Him, and He can't be omnipotent.

FERGUS: These aren't needs I'm describing. These are qualities that define God's essence—we just agreed on them. Look, it is of the sun's essence to fuse atoms of hydrogen, thereby creating light and heat. If the sun didn't radiate light and heat, it wouldn't be the sun. Radiation isn't a need, it is a part of the sun's essence. Loving some different Being is part of God's essence. It's what He does for a living, so to speak.

DAN: But, if He's omnipotent, can't He will Himself to be, to be—?

FERGUS: Something else?

DAN: Yes.

FERGUS: No. Only one being can be omnipotent. You can't have two. If God wills Himself to be something else, He wouldn't be omnipotent. He would cease being God. He'd be a sun that has lost its radiance. Which is something other than a sun.

DAN: Okay. Yes... Okay.

FERGUS: I said God was omni-everything. I didn't say He had an easy time of it.

DAN: So, God—because He didn't have a gin rummy partner—created Adam.

FERGUS: No.

DAN: Then what did God create?

FERGUS: Well, obviously, He created an intelligent Being whom He could love. We've already figured that out. This First Being was no doubt brilliant and lovely. Since it had no other relationship but with God, the First Being had no need of gender. It was sufficient unto itself. It was perfect, perhaps immortal, and maybe just a little bit dull.

DAN: It was neither male nor female?

FERGUS: Rather it was both male and female, Yin and Yang together. The First Being was a whole. It was one complete thing. And it loved God absolutely.

P.A. SPEAKER: Due to frozen signals on the Manhattan Bridge we are being held north of the West 4th Street Station. We expect to be moving shortly and we thank you for your patience.

DAN: Never date a woman who lives in a different borough. It'll be dawn before I get home.

FERGUS: Don't distract me.

DAN: Sorry.

FERGUS: So the First Being loved God absolutely. And God returned that love. But there was something wrong. It didn't feel, you know, natural. See, there was such disproportion between them—God and Being—that the First Being tended to worship, not to love. It couldn't help itself. And worship is love of an enforced kind—not free. Sure the First Being could love God, but like playing golf with your boss, the First Being didn't really enjoy the give-and-take. It was too much in awe.

DAN: So?

FERGUS: Well, God realized that the First Being had been short-changed. It had no equal thing that it could love. So God took the First Being and split it in half. Out of one thing He made two. Male and female, Yin and Yang, Adam and Eve.

DAN: Wait. Hold on. Wait a minute. You're implying that Adam wasn't created first. That Adam and Eve were created at the same time.

FERGUS: I'm not implying. I'm saying. There's a logical necessity to it. Remember the vanilla fudge. If you separate out all the vanilla to make Adam— well then, the fudge that's left must be Eve. The creation of one requires creation of the other.

DAN: Let me get this straight. God created Adam and Eve by splitting an androgynous being in half? It doesn't say that in Genesis.

54

FERGUS: No, it doesn't. The female gender was railroaded and not for the last time. Men wrote the Bible. The writing may have been inspired by God—but not inspired enough to keep men from sticking some self-indulgent male propaganda in. So they let it be known that Adam was the First Being.

DAN: Okay. Even if I grant that. What happens to the scientific explanation?

FERGUS: You mean evolution and all that?

DAN: Uh-huh.

FERGUS: You disappoint me. I didn't think a modern Christian could still have trouble with that. Omnipotent God is a first rate scientist. Of course He created the universe by natural means. Evolution and the Garden of Eden are simply two different ways of looking at the same phenomenon. The scientific way is materialistic and detached. The Garden of Eden way, the mythical way, is passionate and spiritual. But both teach us. The two aren't in conflict with each other—any more than your so-called "real" life and your so-called "dream" life contradict each other. Healing work goes on in dreams. There is symbolic meaning in dreams that transcends reality. Dreams of myth—myths are what we call group dreaming—they can even shed light on science.

DAN: How?

FERGUS: Well, just for one quick example: What did God create Adam from?

DAN: Got me there.

FERGUS: From the dust of the ground and His breath. But Eve was different—different—she was created from what?

DAN: I—oh. Adam's rib. We were talking about it. That's where the spear entered Jesus—where the rib had been taken from Adam.

FERGUS: Good, good. And, presuming Adam to be a normal male, how many ribs did he have? How many ribs do you have?

DAN: No idea.

FERGUS: You and I have twenty-four ribs each. So did Adam. A nice round number. But... But if you took one rib away to make Eve from—then how many ribs would you have?

DAN: Twenty-three, of course.

FERGUS: Yes? And tell me—how many pairs of chromosomes are there in sexual reproduction?

DAN: Is that right? You mean—are there twenty-three?

FERGUS: Twenty-three. Yes. In the middle of boring, unrealistic Genesis, the Genesis that scientists make fun of, God seems to have placed an arithmetical clue that could only be verified after powerful microscopes were invented. The writers of Genesis surely had never seen a chromosome.

DAN: Hmmm. Well... That borders on being clever. But it's probably just a coincidence.

FERGUS: Sure. What else? Sure. But twenty-three is a strange number. Divisible only by one. Not found much in nature. Strange number for the crucial reproductive mechanism to have. Hell, you glance at chromosomes under a microscope, they look like little ribs. But sure it's a coincidence.

DAN: So then Adam's rib is—

FERGUS: Not is. Represents. The rib of Adam in Genesis represents the male sexual chromosome. A sperm with a Y-chromosome if the child is to be male. A sperm with an X-chromosome if it's to be female. From that first X- or Y-chromosome, that first rib, the male's sperm would always decide gender.

DAN: Adam's rib represents the X- or Y-chromosome in the male's sperm. Twenty-four minus one is twenty-three. I have to remember this.

FERGUS: Ah, we're moving. Not fast, but forward at least.

DAN: Am I wrong? If only one chromosome was different then—then Adam and Eve themselves couldn't have been very different.

FERGUS: Bingo. I think Adam and Eve were almost identical twins, that's what I think. Except that one had male sexual equipment. One had female sexual equipment. Mind you, that's saying a lot. I don't minimize it. They had different genital organs and Eve bled every full moon or so. Not only that—on an unconscious level Adam had a female self trapped in the recessive portions of his brain. Vice versa for Eve. Not that Adam and Eve didn't love each other. In fact they loved each other with more innocent rapport than any couple since. They were fascinated with one another. After all Adam and Eve had just had the world's first orgasm together and they wanted to have more.

DAN: Oh?

FERGUS: Yes. In the very first milli-second after God split the First Being in half—immediately, I mean—the first thing that happened was orgasm.

DAN: Why?

FERGUS: God splits the First Being, which is a perfect whole. It's like two powerful magnets getting pulled apart. They struggle to reunite as soon as possible. Or, better yet, it's like a bolt of lightning that slices the air in half. The suddenly heated air expands at supersonic speed. Then the shock wave deteriorates and you get thunder. And the air rushes in to be One again. But when Yin and Yang are bisected by God, when He makes a distinction between male and female—well, then there is no return to the One, to the First Being. When Adam and Eve rushed back together they ran into two physical bodies. Hard, limited and three-dimensional. They could no longer fold themselves into the First Being's safe egg shell. They were separate, they were two Others not a One. Stymied, they made love as their new bodies inclined them to do. Adam and Eve, for a few seconds, recaptured Eden and their lost unity in the human sexual act. In orgasm. And, if they couldn't be One, then they would at least create a child that would involve both of them.

P.A. SPEAKER: This is West 4th Street. Change for the A, C, E, F and Q trains. This train will skip Broadway-Lafayette. Next stop Grand Street.

DAN: But a child isn't the sum of its parents.

FERGUS: Right. The child is different—not least because the child must be male or female. The Yin or Yang, one of them, must predominate. Adam and Eve can't be equal as they once were in the egg.

DAN: In the egg? You mean in the First Being.

FERGUS: Ah, yes. Equal as in the First Being.

DAN: Well, which is it? You seem hesitant.

FERGUS: Ah—I don't want to confuse you now.

DAN: Don't talk down to me. It's not nice.

FERGUS: Okay. The First Being, too, was made in God's image. Was egg-like. Round. Adam and Eve, Yin and Yang, were the yolk and the white of it, so to speak.

DAN: You mean that the First Being was an egg? And the Garden of Eden was also an egg?

FERGUS: Very good. Very good. It can be confusing because we're dealing here with two levels of creation. First there's the creation of Adam and Eve—by God who split the egg-like First Being in half. Then there's the creation of you— by your father, whose sperm split your mother's egg in two. For you, Mom's egg was where you experienced Eden. For Adam and Eve, the First Being, the First Egg, was the Garden of Eden. Genesis carries the myth of man's creation—while, at the same time, with almost the same symbols, Genesis carries the biological truth of your conception and birth. Dan's birth.

DAN: Then... Let me see. Eve was part of the garden slash First Being slash egg. But, at the same time, there was a Garden of Eden in Eve.

FEGUS: Of course. In Eve's ovary. Many eggs, many gardens.

DAN: It's like Chinese boxes. Little Gardens of Eden inside each Garden of Eden and so on. To infinity.

P.A. SPEAKER: Grand Street. Last stop in Manhattan. Dekalb is next.

DAN: Have a slug of Wild Turkey while we're stopped.

FERGUS: I get a little hyper.

DAN: Alcohol is a depressant.

FERGUS: Uh-oh.

DAN: What now?

P.A. SPEAKER: We have a red signal ahead of us. Track crews are clearing ice on the Manhattan Bridge. Thanks for your patience. We will be moving shortly.

FERGUS: Well, at least I'll have time to explain Differentness.

DAN: So it shouldn't be a total loss.

FERGUS: There they were—Adam and Eve—trying to make the best of an unfamiliar scene. They still loved each other, but it was a different kind of love. Not the easy and confident love that they had known before, when they were complementary parts of the primal First Being slash egg. Now their love was emotional, separate, full of tension. And rich with new and very exciting, uh, frictions. The most fascinating thing was this—when Eve knelt to drink she saw her own reflection in the water. And she liked what she saw—because Eve closely resembled Adam, the being she loved. Same thing with Adam. In fact, Adam and Eve were so alike back then—so alike I don't think they fully believed that they were different. Put it this way: Adam and Eve knew that they were "other." But they didn't yet know they were different.

DAN: Other?

FERGUS: Other because they could move independently. Difference, you understand, is a fairly sophisticated concept. It ushers in the whole idea of self. At any rate, being Other, Eve got up early one morning—Adam liked to sleep late—and Eve, moving independently, went for a walk in Eden by herself.

DAN: Uh-oh. Here comes the snake.

FERGUS: Yes, we've gone full circle and we're back there again. But now we know that the serpent isn't a serpent at all. Nor did it do evil. The serpent is—

DAN: The male sperm.

FERGUS: Which looks, under a microscope, just like a serpent—its tail twenty times longer than its head. Not a tadpole at all.

DAN: And we men produce 300,000 of them at one sitting.

FERGUS: Yes, well... Adam and Eve had shared an orgasm together. But conception doesn't happen at orgasm. Conception is something that a woman has to experience herself. Inside herself. The incident that Christians call "The Fall"—when Eve supposedly ate the apple—that's really the moment when Eve accepted the sperm-serpent into her Garden of Eden egg. And life sparked up.

DAN: Adam doesn't have a Garden of Eden in him?

FERGUS: Nope. He doesn't. And probably it's at the moment of conception that Eve realizes, with some shock, that she is different from Adam. And different means unknown. And unknown means incomplete. And incomplete means mortal. The forbidden fruit, the apple, Genesis tells you, brought with it the knowledge of good and evil. Well, Genesis is right. Because the knowledge of good and evil begins with the knowledge of Differentness.

DAN: Give me your *Cliff Notes* definition of Differentness. Again.

FERGUS: Differentness is what God created so that He'd have something or someone other than Himself to love and act upon. Differentness is what God created in the world so that *we* would have something or someone to love and act upon. Other than our egotistic selves. Difference—remember—has no moral value of its own. The table is equal to the chair—though they're different. I am equal to you—though, Lord knows, we're different. Differentness makes love possible—but. But. Big but. Are you listening?

DAN: Haven't much else to do. Yes.

FERGUS: But, if love isn't strong enough to overcome Differentness... or if Differentness is too extreme—as is the case today, I think. Well, then difference becomes the source of comparison and envy and strife. Difference, neutral in itself, turns into a petri dish for evil to grow in. And Eve—who was sharp as a box cutter—Eve suddenly knew all this. She knew that sexual reproduction— expanding geometrically—would in time spread radical difference throughout the world. There wouldn't be enough love to assimilate all Differentness. What else do you think the Tower of Babel story in Genesis is about? It's about the moment—foreseen by Eve—when Differentness became chaos and evil.

DAN: And God stands by?

FERGUS: He sent His Son to bring sameness and unity back into the world— through a shared faith in His grace. It might have worked—but, almost from day one, there was that fatal misunderstanding about Christ's gender in the Church. Christianity split at its center. And, not long after, there wasn't love enough to absorb all the Differentness that gender bias had caused. And schisms began. And racism began. But, whatever the result, God never creates evil, He merely creates Differentness so that we can have others to love. Where the love is inadequate, evil springs up. And meanwhile, back at the ranch—

DAN: Yes?

FERGUS: Eve was having the first ever attack of existential angst. After all, Eve had just found out that she was an *individual*. Adam—always a little slow—was back home sitting in front of the TV waiting for pro football to be invented. How was Eve going to tell Adam? Up to that moment, as far as Eve could see, God and Adam and she were like a molecule of water. Two hydrogen atoms and an oxygen atom bound together forever in one essence, "Waterness." But now Eve saw that the molecular binding was not necessarily permanent. That, under pressure, atom and atom might separate. Worse, Eve knew that she had free will. And with free will you can displease God. Which is scary. Which none of us wants to do.

DAN: Adam had no inkling of all this?

FERGUS: No. But cut him some slack—Adam didn't have a new life growing inside him.

DAN: So Eve has to tell Adam that—that they hadn't been practicing safe sex?

FERGUS: Something along those lines. Yet Adam at first didn't understand Eve—he really had no idea what she was talking about. Still, Adam was a good guy, and he loved Eve, and he very much wanted to make her feel better. So he "ate from the apple" which Eve offered him. By that I mean: Adam listened to what Eve had to say. And, when she finished, Adam was just like Eve. That is: he was one real scared, underconfident individual. Death had come into his life, too. You can't fairly blame Eve for giving Adam the apple. She knew the truth of this new world. He didn't. And they were parents with a child to rear and protect and love. So what do you think Eve said to Adam?

DAN: Oh, you tell me. I tense up on tests.

FERGUS: She told him—well, that he and she were different and might die. And that their child was also different and also might die. And, worse yet, Eve told Adam that their child—Cain—would share a sad and characteristic trait with all of humankind to come. Eve sensed it in her Garden of Eden—that is, Eve sensed it in the egg that was becoming Cain. Eve knew that the female half of Cain had already been driven out by the arrival of Adam's gender-determining sperm. And now that female half—so much beloved—would be imprisoned forever in some attic of Cain's recessive brain.

DAN: Didn't that happen to the original Adam and Eve, too?

FERGUS: No, Dan. Pay attention now. The original Adam and Eve weren't created by sexual reproduction. God made them, you remember, by splitting the First Being in half. Their loss was much less traumatic. In fact it wasn't, strictly speaking, a loss at all. It was more a transformation. This is what happened to the first Adam and Eve: they were separated from the organic chemistry of the First

62

Being slash egg and they were each given a human body. Their orgasms were now local and superficial. Not continuous and total as they had been in the electric protoplasm of the egg. But they still had access to each other. And if Adam missed his female side, well, all he had to do was embrace Eve, who was almost identical to Adam in looks and in the chromosomal code. They probably had a wonderful telepathy between them. Such telepathy as we should have—you and me—with the locked away female selves in our brains.

DAN: So what did they do then?

FERGUS: Says in Genesis: "And they sewed fig leaves together, and made themselves aprons."

DAN: To hide their nakedness.

FERGUS: No. To hide their Differentness.

DAN: But God says to Adam and Eve – am I right?—He says, "How did you two guys know you were naked?"

FERGUS: Dan. Among men and women it is nakedness that betrays difference. Especially for Adam and Eve—who were identical twins except for their private parts. And when they wore fig leaves, there was no visible difference between them at all.

DAN: Vive la same.

FERGUS: So Adam and Eve were driven out of the Garden of Eden—out of the nurturing reproductive system and into the world. A dreadful, traumatic event. But nowhere in Genesis does it say that there were recriminations between them. Adam didn't blame Eve. They loved each other. That love overcame Differentness. As it still can between human beings. It's only in the next generation—with Cain and Abel—that Differentness overcame love and brought evil into existence.

DAN: But, though God drove them out, Eve still had the Garden of Eden inside her? No?

FERGUS: Gardens inside her. One garden for Cain. One garden for Abel. One for Seth. And many, many gardens never fertilized. And so it goes with all women, right down to the garden that nurtured you. You, Adam. And nurtured as well your missing female half, your Eve. Both.

DAN: So us regular guys, secretly we want to wear a tu-tu?

FERGUS: You see? We fell through the trap door again. If you use the terms "male" and" female," you'll get stuck in male-female stereotypes. We have cheapened the Genesis myth by limiting it to stereotypes of maleness and femaleness. As a result women have been relegated to second class citizenship.

DAN: Oh, wow. Now I'll be able to out-Bea Bea. Yes, ma'am, I have seen the light. Sister Eve, she was framed.

FERGUS: Let's act it out. You can play God. It'll be a stretch, but—

DAN: Say what?

FERGUS: You play the part of God. It's an idea I got watching Court TV. "The Trial of Eve." And you get to play God—God as Judge, God as Jury, God as Court Officer. And now—God as Defense Witness. Me? I'm William Kunstler. It's a case that Kunstler would have taken pro bono, don't you think? Anyhow, Kunstler has approached the bench. To everyone's surprise Kunstler asks God Himself if God Himself would appear as a witness for the defense. God agrees. He's perhaps a little overconfident. I—I being Kunstler—I say, "Please take a seat, Your Omnipresence." And you say—as God you say—what?

DAN: Uh. If I'm Omnipresent, I've taken the seat already.

FERGUS: Don't pad your part.

DAN: Gee—why not?—this is the first speaking role I've had on stage in three years. I've always wanted to play the D train. The big time—

FERGUS: Okay, okay. Stop hamming it up.

DAN: Ham it up? Not me. I'm playing God. God's a very understated guy.

64

FERGUS: If you're finished? Yes? Okay, Kunstler steps up and says, "Your Omnibus, would you please straighten something out for me. Precisely what is my client, Eve, accused of?"

DAN: Ah. Well...

FERGUS: Sssst. Disobeyed. Ate the apple. You know. That stuff.

DAN: Oh, yes, ahem. She ate an apple from the tree that gives knowledge of good and evil. What's worse, she disobeyed my order not to do so.

FERGUS: Oh? And why does that trouble you?

DAN: Why? The man asks why. Because I'm God is why. It don't show me no respect.

FERGUS: You mean... Let me see... Do you mean that what Eve did was wrong?

DAN: Of course it's wrong. More than that, it does *bupkis* for my image.

FERGUS: You—do you mean wrong as in "evil" wrong?

DAN: Yes, evil.

FERGUS: In that case, your Honor, I move that the charge be dismissed. My client, Eve, you see—she had no knowledge of good or evil *until after she ate the apple*. Guilt is based on the ability to distinguish good from evil at the moment that a so-called crime is committed. My client is therefore innocent.

DAN: Oh, nifty. That beats the Twinkie defense.

FERGUS: Of course Eve did tempt Adam.

DAN: Yeah. What about that?

FERGUS: Well, temptation is just a misdemeanor, Your Honor. Shall we plea bargain down to, say, a fifty dollar fine and ten days' community service? Frankly, Your Honor, that Fall of Man and Original Sin stuff—it would never fly in the appellate court.

DAN: Yeah. I guess. It doesn't look good for God to have His decisions overturned.

FERGUS: So Adam and Eve, by the particular logic of Genesis itself, were innocent. Hey. We're on our way again. Not going very fast, though. What's the state of our liquid rations?

DAN: Two decent-size swigs, I figure. One for you. One for me. I'll go first.

FERGUS: Take it easy—you've got more at home.

DAN: Relax. I left you plenty. Here.

FERGUS: Mmmm. Think of all the calories I'm getting. Mmmm. Thank you, Daniel. Mmmm. I can feel my luck changing, as we speak.

DAN: So Eve got a bum rap?

FERGUS: Oh, heck, it's human enough. There was a lot of evil in the world— back when Genesis was first hitting the newsstands. No one ever wants to blame God. An Almighty One that does evil? Uh-uh. That way madness lies. Better to invent the concept of Original Sin, the Fall, the Serpent and then load all the blame on ourselves. We feel comfortable with guilt. But... On the other hand— gosh, let's not go overboard with this blame stuff. No need for all of us to do hard time—is there? Why not write it up so the major blame falls on Eve. And, by descent, on all women. They will lie forever in the shadow of the male's moral superiority. Backed up, if necessary, by his physical strength, which at least is real.

DAN: The Manhattan Bridge. Have we only gotten that far? Mother's gonna worry.

FERGUS: Sleet's stopped, I think.

DAN: Should pick up speed once we get across. Unless the elevated parts of the track in Brooklyn have icing problems, too. Oh, great. I should keep my mouth shut. Stopped again.

FERGUS: Wind is still terrific.

DAN: Lookit that track crew. They must be miserable with the cold.

FERGUS: You'd be surprised what people can get used to.

DAN: Yeah, maybe. In fact I was going to ask you. The weather here being what it is—why don't you hop a freight to Miami?

FERGUS: What? And leave show business? Dan. Come over to the window here.

DAN: Yeah? I've seen it. I take the D train at least three times a week.

FERGUS: The Statue of Liberty. Just there. Past the Brooklyn Bridge.

DAN: Sure enough. Hmmm. Didn't realize you could see so far.

FERGUS: It amazes me. We're in the underground and suddenly we can see New York Harbor and all of Europe implied behind it.

DAN: The Big Apple.

FERGUS: Yeah. Why do they call it that?

DAN: Big Apple? I dunno.

FERGUS: Big Diamond. Big Rip-Off. Those I could understand. But Apple? Kind of inappropriate, isn't it? Kind of a rather rustic name for a major urban center. Don't you think?

DAN: What? Is this leading somewhere? Apple... Oh, boy. Now he's gonna tell me all of New York City lies in my mother's left ovary.

FERGUS: Ha! Not yet.

DAN: So what's it stand for, Big Apple?

FERGUS: You're asking me? I don't know. Maybe something's supposed to happen here.

DAN: What? What? You're spooking me with all this apple and garden stuff. It's all symbolism, with no science behind it.

FERGUS: Oh? Science has its myths, too. What about the apple that fell in Newton's garden? From that apple all modern thinking in physics was conceived. Science and myth overlap. Different apples in different gardens. Two ways of seeing the same eternity. The Falling Apple and the Apple of the Fall.

DAN: That is a weird coincidence.

FERGUS: Look at all the lights. Every one of them stands for someone who's different from you. Different from me. One of these days all that fierce variety will short circuit the universe.

P.A. SPEAKER: We should be moving soon. Dekalb Avenue is next.

FERGUS: Eventually Differentness, overwhelming love, becomes the topsoil in which prejudice and jealousy and war begin to grow. The topsoil itself is innocent. God lets us, by our free will, He lets us plant whatever we want.

DAN: Murder and muggings. Slander and fraud.

FERGUS: Oh, that's only the most obvious effect of Differentness. The really important effect is much more subtle, much more pervasive than all that.

DAN: I'm afraid to ask.

FERGUS: Can't you tell? Without Differentness there could be no beauty in the world. Nor any noble tragedy. That's the Catch 22.

DAN: No beauty? How do you mean?

FERGUS: Beauty and all forms of human excellence, they force us to make distinctions. Which lead to difference. By how much this one women is the most beautiful, by that amount the beauty of all other women is reduced. By how brilliantly Shakespeare wrote, my writing and your writing will be that much diminished.

DAN: Hmmm.

FERGUS: Only those whose love is torrential and unqualified—only absolute love like that can overcome Differentness. But men and women who show such radiant love are called saints. I don't know about you—me, I'm not one of them. Saints are set aside as being holy, which holiness, in turn, makes you and me seem less good, less loving. So Differentness, even in the service of good, will tend to divide and subdivide us.

DAN: Yeah, really good people are irritating.

P.A. SPEAKER: DeKalb Avenue. Step up. Atlantic Avenue is next.

DAN: But isn't Differentness politically correct? Individualism gets good PR these days.

FERGUS: Yes. But there is a line between individualism, which is good, and alienation, which is self-loving and corrupt. The socio-political-ethnic-religious structures which nourished sameness are collapsing. Nation fragments into parties, party into ethnic groups, group into neighborhoods, neighborhood into gangs, which fragment into families, which are broken to start with—which all leaves us with the unattached individual—who has no particular allegiance to anything. Even Communism, with all its apparatus of police state terrorism, Communism could not defuse or contain Differentness.

DAN: Yugoslavia.

FERGUS: Yes. We celebrate diversity. Our mayors praise the "gorgeous mosaic" of their cities. But instead of praising diversity, instead we should be asking, "Just how much more Differentness can this planet take before no inhabitant is recognizable to another inhabitant." Because then love will be paralyzed.

DAN: How so?

FERGUS: Because you cannot love what you don't recognize. If you don't know what a thing is, you can't even understand how it differs from you. And you certainly won't know how to love it or do it any good. Help it, heal it, become part of it. And that's what Hell is.

DAN: Hell?

FERGUS: Hell, as I imagine it, is Differentness at critical mass. A place where no thing can resemble any other thing at all. Where likeness is dissolved in endless variation without a theme. It is absolute terror. Even our body parts no longer have a familiar form. Pain and pleasure are interchangeable. Hell is to be completely alone among an infinite number of unrecognizable things. Life in a mad abstract-expressionist landscape. Where no thing has a name.

DAN: Enough. I get your drift. I had an acid trip like that once. The worst time of my life.

P.A. SPEAKER: Atlantic Avenue. Seventh Avenue next.

FERGUS: Well, the pre-Christian world must've been like that, a hellish acid trip. Talk about wonderful diversity. And so God sent Jesus to spread a little sameness around. Egyptians, Persians, Illyrians, people from the Caucasus, Nubians and so forth. Only Rome kept the Western World from disintegrating entirely. Three hundred years later, under Constantine, Christianity became the imperial religion. And there was some reliable sameness in the world.

DAN: Yeah, reliable. Schism and sect and holy war. I read where one early Christian group refused to be martyred at the same end of the Coliseum with some other Christian group they disagreed with. I mean, if you can't be forgiving when you're about to be turned into a lion's lunch meat—

P.A. SPEAKER: Seventh Avenue. This train will bypass both the Prospect Park Station and the station at Parkside. Church Avenue is next.

DAN: We should be out of the tunnel soon.

FERGUS: You were saying?

DAN: Unh. Oh. Christianity has hardly been a binding force.

FERGUS: Inquisitions, crusades. Yes. It's not pretty. Still, in the West anyway, just about everyone shared at least one fairly complex idea. Namely: that a man, who happened also to be Almighty God, voluntarily died on the cross to redeem man's sinful nature. There had never been such a widespread understanding of a single spiritual principle before. A single spiritual drama. A great sameness.

DAN: Well, maybe, but...

FERGUS: Jesus was sent here to reduce Differentness—and to do it through love. What after all, are His two great commandments?

DAN: Mmmm?

FERGUS: Well?

DAN: Oh, you're asking *me*? I thought it was one of your many rhetorical questions. So. Ah. Yes. "Love God with all your heart," et cetera. And. And, you know...

FERGUS: "Love thy neighbor as thyself." It's the most powerful and comprehensive ethical statement in all scripture.

DAN: I was just gonna say that. You didn't give me time.

P.A. SPEAKER: Church Avenue. Beverley Road is next.

FERGUS: "Love thy neighbor as thyself." "Neighbor," for one, is an all-inclusive term. I've had plenty of neighbors—most of them I've never even spoken to. Now that I'm on the street, I'm kind of a universal neighbor.

DAN: Look, I try to give the homeless a buck or two every day I'm in town.

FERGUS: No. No. This isn't some complex guilt trip. Jesus isn't talking about money. He's talking about an act of imagination that reduces Differentness. The most important words are not "Love thy neighbor." The most important words are "as thyself." For instance, you were scared by that black kid back on 116th Street—

DAN: Wait one dang minute here. Don't make me out to be a racist. I'm not. I got mugged and I'm a little gun shy.

FERGUS: No one's calling you a racist. What Jesus means is this. When a sixteen year-old black boy enters a subway car, he frightens you with his

Differentness. Differentness, unmitigated by love, is scary. But how should we generate the necessary love? By loving because we're Christian? Because Christians ought to love any sixteen year-old *in spite of* his blackness? No. That's condescension, not love. Should we love him because he, like us, eats, sleeps and dies? No, crocodiles and hyenas share those traits. No. You should love that teen-ager, "as thyself." As if you yourself were black, sixteen, and bitterly disheartened because—whenever you entered a subway car—every single white person watched you. Every single one. And the body language changed. Yes, in every single person. And they couldn't help themselves. No, because they were scared out of their gourds. Really scared. Really. And you—Mr. Sixteen Year-old—you have done this—and with schoolbooks under your arm no less. No matter what you achieve in your life—good or bad—this will most certainly not change. So, from feeling lonely and outcast, one day you start enjoying that body language shift. You start thinking, maybe you'd like a little *more* shift. A little *more* respect. Well, I tell ya, Dan—I don't blame him. I mean, is that the way to live a life? Feel it for a moment, you're an actor, fer gosh sake. Try *feeling* the first ten people you meet in a day.

DAN: Fergus, that was eloquent. And no doubt there's a lot of human truth in what you say. But... I'm not trying to be flip or anything, but—what you've got in mind is a helluva lot of work.

FERGUS: Well, sure it is. Once established, its hard to root Differentness out. And, anyway, you wouldn't want to root it all out. But the radical Differentness, the dangerous Differentness, something has to be done about that. What we need are great acts of empathy. The willing suspension of our personality. To *be* someone else. To paraphrase Jesus, "Where your identity is, there will your heart be also."

P.A. SPEAKER: This is Beverley. Next stop Cortelyou Road.

DAN: Lots of luck. You make a persuasive case. But the average guy—guys who own all the dingy backyards we're passing now. Those guys just want a not-too-humiliating life—without having to commit a major felony to pay for it.

FERGUS: Right. But imagine—just as an example—imagine what it's like to live with your bedroom window up against the D train track. Empathize. Think what acoustical adjustment it would require—not to hear those blasts of crashing metal all day long—empathize.

DAN: Listen. You want Differentness? Today I took four cabs in the city. One driver was a 27 year-old Sikh. One was a black woman from Jamaica. One was a 70 year-old Jewish guy who kept his false teeth in a Tupperware bowl on the dashboard. In case he had to speak with you. The fourth one was... I don't remember—but you can be sure he was different. To, like, empathize with them all—I'd have to hire an off-Broadway theatre.

FERGUS: Oh, I know. I know. I am myself almost impossible to empathize with. No. That's why I think we have to heal the critical difference first—the difference that lies in gender. Especially gender difference in the Christian churches. So the churches can again be a benevolent source of sameness. At least in the West.

DAN: Yes, but...

P.A. SPEAKER: This is Cortelyou Road. Because of track repair we will be bypassing Newkirk Avenue. Passengers for Newkirk should get off at Avenue H and change for the westbound D. Avenue H next.

DAN: But what about the Catholics' Virgin Mary?

FERGUS: Well, first of all, nothing that I say is meant to cast dishonour on that exquisite Lady. She is pure, holy, comforting and efficacious in the way of miracles. The church, after a while, sensing female unrest, gave the Virgin Mary to women. So that they could be Her royal maids-in-waiting. But—

DAN: I was waiting for the "but—"

FERGUS: But the Virgin is not, nor never can be, the female counterpart of Jesus, Son of Man. And without that exact female counterpart the Word was made male flesh only—and we are broken in half. The Incarnation becomes a less than universal moment. Created by males for the redemption of males.

DAN: What did Bea tell me? A group of—oh, some Protestant branch, it doesn't matter—anyhow the women of this branch or sect went on a retreat to worship the Goddess Sophia or something.

FERGUS: Sophia, wisdom. She's not a goddess, she's a venerable aspect of the Godhead. She's the personification of Divine Wisdom. But she, too, isn't Jesus's counterpart.

DAN: So—

FERGUS: The point is this: I'd rather have a Christ Who contains two perfect and equal genders in Him—than the opposite. The opposite being a church with a different god or goddess for each gender. That would be hard to get used to. Even for an Episcopalian. But—

DAN: But?

FERGUS: But let's assume the churches accepted a Christ Who had both genders. There is, I assure you, nothing in traditional theology to prevent the churches from doing so—nothing. In fact, during the high Middle Ages, it was common for certain monastic orders to depict Jesus as mother as well as father. The great monastic, St. Bernard of Clairvaux, said, "Suck not so much the wounds as the breasts of the Crucified. He will be your mother and you will be His son." St. Bernard had no problem with a male-female Christ, why should we? It doesn't threaten traditional theology, it merely elaborates on that theology. And it would heal the congregations. For the first time men and women would be equal in Christ.

DAN: Suck Jesus's breasts? Come on, Fergus. That's a bit much, even for you. I don't claim to be an expert—I'm a dolt and a pushover for a glib guy like you—

74

but even I know better than that. No way the church was talking about Jesus's um, breasts.

FERGUS: You don't believe me? Let's go to the public library. Let's go right now. In the twelfth century, besides St. Bernard, there was William of St. Thierry, Anselm of Canterbury—I can show you dozens of references to Jesus's milk. In a book called *Jesus As Mother* by Caroline Walker Bynum. And that's not all—

DAN: The problem with you, friend—your problem is you know too damn much. Or you think you know too damn much. If we had a real theologian here—

FERGUS: Real theologian? Grow up. Think for yourself, why don't you? Or do you need an authority figure to validate your own common sense?

DAN: No, I don't need an authority figure—look, I'm tired and I don't like being pushed into a corner. I have a right to my own ideas—

FERGUS: And what are those?

P.A. SPEAKER: This is Avenue H. Avenue J next.

FERGUS: Well. What are your ideas?

DAN: Don't get so smug. My ideas are my ideas. If your Eden in the ovary theory is such hot stuff, why haven't you written it up as a book? Why hasn't anyone published it?

FERGUS: Because it's just come to me—over the last three months. Being out on the street kind of returns you to the basics. Like: "What is this stupid life all about, anyway?" I'd been taken down a peg—and maybe I needed that.

DAN: Oh, I see. Just because you're going through the change of life—the rest of us have to suffer right along with you. But maybe it's just you. You screwed up. It doesn't mean the whole world needs a new cosmology.

FERGUS: I know what kicked this off.

DAN: Kicked what off?

FERGUS: This righteous fit of yours.

DAN: Jesus The Nursing Mother is what did it.

FERGUS: Bull. It's when I started talking about your female half—that's when I hit a sore spot.

DAN: Oh, please, enough of this New Age sensitivity. I hear it all the time.

FERGUS: Most men are afraid to let the female half of their brain, let it have freedom to operate. They're afraid, if they do that, the little lady inside, she'll reach down and grab the steering wheel. And you'll crash. But, the joke is, you're utterly dependent on your female self already.

DAN: Am I really?

FERGUS: Jesus, Mary and Joseph—you told me you were an actor, didn't you? Don't tell me any decent actor isn't aware of his feminine traits. Or aren't you a decent actor?

DAN: I act just fine, thank you.

FERGUS: Well, yes. I'm sure you do.

DAN: Oh, butter wouldn't melt in your mouth, would it? Listen, feminine traits are one thing. I'm not ashamed to acknowledge mine. But, yes, I'm not so comfortable with this female half idea. I don't know what it means. Some kind of Tinkerbell inside my brain sprinkling Disney Dust around? What?

FERGUS: Well...

P.A. SPEAKER: This is Avenue J. Step in. Avenue M is next.

FERGUS: Look, your girlfriend is a strong woman—partly that's what draws you to her. Remember, women have to deal with their male halves, too. Their Yang part. In general, though, it's easier for women. They haven't got as much at stake in being female—as men have in being male. Probably because political, social and economic power lies with the male. The Yang.

DAN: Gobbledy-gook.

FERGUS: Part of you—the female, the Yin half—would like Bea to take care of you.

DAN: Nonsense.

FERGUS: No, it isn't. Because of the way our society is structured—and it's structured that way because men are physically stronger—and because women are designed for motherhood—because of our male-oriented culture, females are scavenged, cannibalized to make men stronger.

DAN: What's that supposed to mean?

FERGUS: He still lives with his mother at age—what are you, 35 or so?—he still lives with his mother and he doesn't know what that means. Does she make your bed?

DAN: Hey, it gives her something to do.

FERGUS: She being incapable of doing something for herself. And I bet there was a sister, too. I bet you had a sister.

DAN: I have a sister.

FERGUS: And what does she do?

DAN: She does fine. She's married with two kids.

FERGUS: What college did she go to?

DAN: She didn't. She wasn't interested in academics.

FERGUS: Couldn't see the sense of preparing herself for a lousy career in a male-dominated world. Huh? So the surplus resources were allocated to you.

DAN: Oh, lay off.

FERGUS: And the topless dancers and the one-night stands that validated you.

DAN: Look. Enough. I'm not on trial here. My life isn't yours to judge. Let's just let it alone. You got some nerve, you with the younger woman bimbo—

FERGUS: All right, I went too far.

DAN: Damn right you did. And I've had it. I can see why you're homeless.

FERGUS: All right. All right. I get a little desperate sometimes. I'm like the Ancient Mariner.

DAN: And I'm tired. So. Enough. You've made your point. Just shut up while you're ahead.

FERGUS: All right. All right.

P.A. SPEAKER: This is Avenue M. Watch the doors. Kings Highway is next. This is Kings Highway. Watch the doors. Next stop Avenue U.

FERGUS: Wind seems to have blown itself out.

DAN: Mmmm.

P.A. SPEAKER: Avenue U. Watch your step.

FERGUS: Stars. Cleared up. Hope it gets warmer. Haven't been to Coney in years. Maybe I'll dip my foot in the Atlantic. Maybe that'll change my luck.

DAN: Mmmm.

P.A. SPEAKER: This is Neck Road. Watch the doors. Next is Sheepshead Bay.

FERGUS: Listen, you can have the money back. Here it is.

DAN: Oh, please.

FERGUS: No. It's reasonable. You didn't get what you paid for.

DAN: Please. It was all very interesting.

FERGUS: But I shouldn't have gotten personal. You told me things in confidence and I used them against you. That was contemptible of me. I apologize for it.

DAN: Accepted.

FERGUS: Here. Take it back.

DAN: Look, I can afford the money. Let it alone. Just let it alone.

FERGUS: All right. All right.

P.A. SPEAKER: Sheepshead Bay. Doors closing. Brighton Beach is next.

DAN: Look, there's no way I can put you up for the night, I simply can't. Call it what you will, I can't.

FERGUS: Huh?

DAN: I would, but I can't. Put you up for the night. It's impossible, so there's no sense getting into it.

FERGUS: You think I—

DAN: We've got only a two-bedroom condo. And my mother is—at her age— she gets nervous.

FERGUS: Hey, I'm doing fine. I've adapted to being homeless rather well, I think. I mean, I haven't starved. I haven't been immolated. I haven't lost anything to frostbite. I'm sorta, in a way, well, sorta proud of it.

DAN: My mother—

FERGUS: Oh. I wouldn't inflict myself on her. I have some dignity left. No, I'll be fine. With what you gave me, I can look forward to a good meal tonight. Maybe even a shower.

DAN: That "Love thy neighbor" stuff got a bit thick. You really troweled it on.

FERGUS: Ho, I wasn't—

DAN: I can relate to your situation. I can wish you better times. And gladly. But I don't see how I'm responsible. I just don't.

FERGUS: Did I ever say you were responsible?

DAN: Well, in a sense, we all are.

FERGUS: I don't know about "we." I don't know about "all." I know about you. You are not responsible for me. And, anyhow, a literal Christian—someone who took Jesus literally—that person couldn't go the bodega for a six-pack. He'd get sidetracked by poverty and despair before he could go half a block. He'd be paralyzed, the culture would be paralyzed.

DAN: I suppose.

FERGUS: But you can do something for me.

DAN: Oh?

FERGUS: Let me finish my Jesus spiel. It's not often I get a chance to tell the whole thing from beginning to end. Almost never with an intelligent audience.

DAN: Sure. Ah, how much more is there?

FERGUS: Just enough. We need to come full circle again. We've gone from The spear and the crucifixion to the Garden of Eden. Now it's time we returned to Golgotha. And closed the circuit, you might say.

DAN: Is ten dollars a fair price?

FERGUS: No, no. You paid for this.

DAN: Here. Take.

FERGUS: Haven't you noticed? You and me, we're not clear on the subject of money right now.

DAN: Maybe you're right.

FERGUS: Okay, then. Here goes.

DAN: Okay.

P.A. SPEAKER: This is Sheepshead Bay. Watch your step. Ocean Parkway will be next.

FERGUS: Let me tell you how all this came to me. There's an old carol called, "Jesus Christ the Apple Tree." Beautiful. Unknown composer. Anyhow, one day I was going over the Garden of Eden stuff and this carol kept popping into my head. And all at once I said to myself, why is he, the unknown composer, why is he calling Jesus "the apple tree?" Why "apple tree?"

DAN: Symbol of fertility?

FERGUS: I thought of that. But then I also thought, "Hey, it's traditional to say that Jesus was hanged on a tree at the crucifixion." And it's also commonplace, as we know, to say that Jesus was "Second Adam." So I can take it for granted that—symbolically at least—there are powerful references to the Garden of Eden in the crucifixion. And vice versa. In fact the two events might be the same event—seen through glasses of different magnification, so to speak. And different color. And different polarity.

DAN: The same event?

FERGUS: Well, I've shown you how the crucifixion and the Garden intersect. God took Adam's rib—image of the gender chromosome—and created Eve from it. On Golgotha the spear, like a surgeon's scalpel, enters Jesus's side and grafts the rib back into place. Jesus becomes One again, male and female reunited together. That is: symbolically He becomes the perfect, undifferent First Being— as that First Being was before God split it into Yin and Yang, red and blue, Adam and Eve. So Jesus is healed. And then where does He go?

DAN: To His Father.

FERGUS: Before that.

DAN: Oh. To hell. Descends.

FERGUS: And how do we define hell?

DAN: A place where you don't recognize anything. And you can't love what you don't know.

FERGUS: Right. Everything is different. Radically different. But Jesus, entering Hell, contains all possible variation. He is male-female, obverse-reverse, Yin and Yang—He represents the perfect First Being. The One. And that perfect First Being is entirely Love. And, since it is entirely Love, the First Being can recognize everything in Hell. And, as soon as it is recognized, known, named, then Hell is destroyed. "Hell took a body and met God face to face," says St. John

Chrysostom. "It took earth and encountered Heaven, it took that which was seen and fell upon the unseen. Oh, Death, where is thy sting? Oh, Hell, where is thy victory?" In Hell Differentness could find no place to pry Jesus open. He was no longer wounded by a missing gender half—as we still are. He was the perfect One. In Hell Jesus was Every-Place-he-Same where every place was different. Jesus didn't rise from Hell. Hell shot Him the heck out of there before Hell was demolished by His presence. Before it was fully known.

DAN: I like that.

P.A. SPEAKER: This is Ocean Parkway. Watch the doors. West 8th Street next.

DAN: But this hermaphrodite Christ—

FERGUS: No. No. Please don't misquote me on that. I never said that Jesus was a hermaphrodite. And He isn't. I never said that Jesus was androgynous. And He isn't. He's not a bisexual either. And here, mind you, I take my thinking from textbook Christian theology. Textbook theology insists that Jesus in Bethlehem and Jesus in Jerusalem and Jesus on the cross were all perfect man. And, at the same time, they were all perfect God. No contradiction. That's the heart of the Christian faith. But. But. But.

DAN: Take it easy. Don't give yourself a hernia.

FERGUS: But. But since Jesus as God is omniscient, since He must have a perfect memory, He must—He must—He must also remember perfectly that glorious Eden time in the Virgin Mary's egg. When He had the potential to be complete woman and complete man. When He held within Him the Yin and the Yang in equal measure. When, from His female genetic message He could envision—no, He could sense—no, He could *experience*—He could experience menstrual pain and mother love.

DAN: I see what you're after.

FERGUS: Moreover, Jesus had free and complete access to His feminine side, the Yin side, of His brain. I'd guess that's where His miraculous powers came from. It makes sense. No theologian can deny that Jesus knew and remembered His female half in the egg—unless that theologian is willing to deny Jesus's omniscience. Sperm are male or female. The egg is male *and* female. Omniscient God knew both gender states. And could promise atonement for all of us because His sacrifice was absolute. Amen.

DAN: Is that it?

FERGUS: For now. That's enough for now. Why? You want a refund?

DAN: No. God, no.

FERGUS: I'm hoarse from yelling.

DAN: You spoke longer than Fidel Castro does on May Day.

P.A. SPEAKER: West 8th Street. Watch the doors. Next and last stop, Stillwell Avenue, Coney Island.

FERGUS: So, did I convince you?

DAN: I don't know. It gives me plenty to think about.

FERGUS: I realize that. It's a lot to digest at one sitting. But keep it alive in your head. Kick the thing around. It'll grow on you.

DAN: Well, I will.

FERGUS: Hey, the Atlantic Ocean. I didn't realize you could see the Atlantic ocean from a D train. Or I forgot.

DAN: Tankers out there.

FERGUS: Maybe I'll go down to the ocean and dabble my feet.

DAN: I wouldn't recommend it.

FERGUS: Cold, huh? Well, still what a rare opportunity. Step into the underground and come out on the mighty ocean. It would be a waste not to take advantage of it.

DAN: Under that boardwalk—you don't know what's under there. Some kind of bottom feeder might jump out with a knife.

FERGUS: Then come with me.

DAN: I've got a six block walk west.

FERGUS: Just for a few minutes. Be a sport. Since you're not putting me up.

DAN: Oh, screw you.

FERGUS: I'm only kidding. But I would like to walk on the beach. The amphibian inside me calls.

DAN: First see how hard the wind is blowing.

FERGUS: You lived here as a kid? You lived inside an amusement park?

DAN: Worked the games every summer. "Hey, Pal. Prove you're a man. Win the lady a three foot tall Minnie Mouse doll. Just throw two baseballs through the hanging toilet seat."

FERGUS: Sounds authentic.

DAN: Hey, I'm an actor. And, well, some nights you could make real good money. Since I lived in the neighborhood anyway. But this place is not an amusement park. Disney makes amusement parks. Coney is—and I love it, mind you—Coney is… I don't know. The red light district of the soul. Sordid. But sordid with a sense of humor. An innocent kind of sordidness.

FERGUS: Where everyone knows they're being ripped off—and no hard feelings.

P.A. SPEAKER: Stillwell Avenue. Last stop.

FERGUS: Don't walk too fast now. I'm pretty good once I get my bad foot in rhythm. It's not very windy up here. Oh, the ramp. I remember this long ramp down. Last time I was here must've been in the early '70s.

84

DAN: Ssst, Fergus. See him? The black kid who's been following us. He just passed us going down the ramp.

FERGUS: Are you sure?

DAN: Of course I am. Same orange tartan hood on his jacket. I was right. He was setting us up to be mugged.

FERGUS: Yeah? If his trade was mugging, why didn't he get back on the train? Who can he mug here? A seagull? Look. Someone was waiting in a car to pick him up.

DAN: I'll be damned.

FERGUS: Nathan's. The cholesterol capital of the world. Surf Avenue. It's warmer here. The Boardwalk's not even a block away. Come on.

DAN: When we get to the open beach it'll blow up. You watch.

FERGUS: Fifteen minutes, that's all. Come. Oh, there's the bumper car place. What I used to do was, I'd wait for some pretty girl to buy a ticket. Then I'd get a car and smack her around whenever I could. With a smile on my face.

DAN: That wasn't very nice.

FERGUS: No, but it was cheaper than therapy. I don't want you thinking that I was being "holier than thou" back there. We all have our sins against the ladies. All men do.

DAN: Scavenged? Is that the word you used?

FERGUS: Yes. Cannibalized. Men—especially men of genius—they're the product of female energy, female life force channeled into them. The great question is—"Are the complete works of William Shakespeare worth the suffering and degradation of a single woman?"

DAN: What did Shakespeare do to women?

FERGUS: Nothing more than any other man. He was the product of his age. The very best product. The very best age. Yet it was an age based, as most ages have been, on the programmatic exploitation of women. They couldn't even appear on stage.

DAN: "Are the complete works of—" Well, I'd hate to lose *King Lear*... Just how badly is this hypothetical woman suffering?

FERGUS: You're not allowed to ask that. It's enough for you to know that she suffers. You can't judge the degree of another's pain. And, by the way, she isn't hypothetical. She exists and she existed—and I'm afraid she'll continue to exist. In return men produce very few *King Lears*.

DAN: So what's the answer to your question?

FERGUS: You can ask that? There's only one possible answer. Good grief, Dan. You embarrass me.

DAN: Oh.

FERGUS: Lookit this place—it's as scuzzy as a tenement airshaft. Yet, talk about mystical. The parachute jump—looks like the metal skeleton for a mushroom cloud. And the Wonder Wheel and all the little wheels. And the peculiar sway-backed curves of the roller coasters. There's probably some secret and potent diagram in the Kabala that looks like Coney Island.

DAN: Don't talk so much. Move. It's cold as a space walk out here.

FERGUS: Seagulls, wonk-wonk-wonk. The most ironic sound in all nature.

DAN: Move.

FERGUS: Wish we hadn't finished the Wild Turkey.

DAN: So do I. No, not under the boardwalk, let's take the ramp over it. No telling what kind of drug deal's going on down there.

FERGUS: Well, look at that. What a prospect. The rind of the sun coming up in the east. And yet still dark enough in the west to see the stars. What do you think about—I mean, when you see the stars?

DAN: I think it's warmer up there than it is down here.

FERGUS: The sand. I want to walk in the sand. And touch the ocean.

DAN: I was afraid of that. Okay, come. Can you believe that woman, jogging in weather like this? Watch it here, the steps are narrow.

FERGUS: Uh-oh, sand.

DAN: That's what they call it.

FERGUS: No, in my sneaker. Full of holes. My foot's gonna sound like a maraca all day.

DAN: Just don't kick any on me.

FERGUS: You didn't answer my question—the stars. What d'you think about when you see the stars?

DAN: I dunno. My own insignificance, I guess.

FERGUS: Right. And yet—here I sound an optimistic note for a change—and yet a single human choice for good here on earth is worth all the galaxies. I can fit nebulas into my brain. So can you. But the whirling, wild gases out there are insensate. They can't love God. Or hate Him. That's what Jesus learned here— and informed His Father of. Our pain. And the dreadful limitations of our flesh. And everpresent death. "Truly," He must've said to God, "one man's 'little, nameless, unremembered acts of kindness and of love' are worth the angels' choir."

DAN: If you say so.

FERGUS: The angels are boring to Him. We are His pleasure.

DAN: I'm glad to hear it. Stick your toe in the water. There. Now let's get going.

FERGUS: Wait.

DAN: What're you doing? Put that back on.

FERGUS: I want you to do me a favor. Trade coats.

DAN: What? Are you insane?

FERGUS: Hurry. Take your coat off, I'm freezing. Hurry.

DAN: Take my coat off—

FERGUS: Yes. Yes. Hurry. It's a good deal really. This is a better coat. Just go and get it dry-cleaned.

DAN: No.

FERGUS: Your coat is new, it doesn't have mozzarella on it. It'll give me a chance at job interviews.

DAN: But I can't stand the stink.

FERGUS: What about me? You think I enjoy that smell? I don't. I was a very fastidious man, when last I was a man.

DAN: Fergus—

FERGUS: I'm freezing.

DAN: Damn it all. Here.

FERGUS: Thank you, thank you. Now put mine on.

DAN: No.

FERGUS: It's pointless if you don't.

DAN: What's pointless?

FERGUS: The whole damn project's pointless. This exchange of you and me.

DAN: Okay, I get it. I get it, and I don't have to put your coat on.

FERGUS: Yes, you do. Put it on, your teeth are chattering.

DAN: Nuts. Oh, hell. There, are you satisfied? God what a rancid stench.

FERGUS: Really something, isn't it? That coat hasn't been off my back in three months.

DAN: Spare me the gory details. Let's get back.

FERGUS: No. You go. Sun's almost up. Nobody's going to mug me in daylight. I want to walk along the beach.

DAN: In this weather? You're crazy. Come with me.

FERGUS: I'll be all right. It's just as cold in the city. And in the city I'm always out of place. A man walking by the ocean isn't homeless. It's good for my self-esteem.

DAN: Okay. You're a grown up, you know what you're doing. Here's my card. Give me a couple of days to clean this, then call.

FERGUS: Right, we'll do lunch. Tell your people to get in touch with my people.

DAN: You're a real character.

FERGUS: Yeah, I know. Let me give you a blessing. In the name of The Father and of The Son and of The Holy Spirit. Which is She in God.

DAN: She?

FERGUS: Of course. The Holy Spirit is the female aspect of the Godhead. What else? In fact, I can't understand why women haven't appropriated the Holy Spirit long before this. It was always there for the taking. She was always there.

DAN: The Holy Spirit is female?

FERGUS: You're surprised?

DAN: But that would make The Holy Spirit—what?

FERGUS: Jesus's sister.

DAN: Jesus's sister?

FERGUS: Uh-huh. Well, you better be moving. Thanks for everything. And don't get too comfortable with my coat.

DAN: So long.

FERGUS: So long.

[*FERGUS turns, He begins limping southeast along the shoreline. DAN watches him for a moment, but FERGUS doesn't glance back.*

After a moment DAN catches a whiff of himself. He turns quickly and begins running toward the stairs, kicking up sand behind him. Once across the boardwalk—out of FERGUS'S view—he rips the coat off.

The money he gave FERGUS falls out of the left hand coat pocket.

DAN rushes back to the boardwalk, shouting, waving, the money held high. But he can see no sign of FERGUS. For a long moment DAN stares at the shoreline. Then, deflated, he starts walking toward his home.

It is almost full dawn now.]

PART TWO

THE THEOPHYSICAL UNIVERSE

P.A. SPEAKER: This is a Manhattan-bound D train. Watch the doors. Next stop West 8th Street, New York Aquarium.

FEMALE VOICE: Good afternoon, sir. It's hot out there today, on the beach, isn't it?

DAN: Not now, thanks. I haven't got any loose change right now. Sorry.

FEMALE VOICE: I hate to trouble you, sir. I know you've got your own problems—

DAN: Lady, please.

FEMALE VOICE: I was burned out last month. My apartment was burned out. If you could spare a dollar or two—

DAN: Please. I'm sure there's an appropriate social service agency. I'm sure they'll help you.

FEMALE VOICE: You mean a city shelter? For a woman my age, pardon me, a woman my age wouldn't last two minutes in a city shelter. That's the truth.

DAN: Here. All right, here. That's all I've got—a token and two quarters. There.

FEMALE VOICE: Thank you. God bless and thank you.

DAN: It's all I can spare now.

FEMALE VOICE: Think I'll sit down. Is it okay if I sit down?

DAN: Uh.

P.A. SPEAKER: West 8th Street. Ocean Parkway next.

FEMALE VOICE: You know what I'd like? You've been very generous, but you know what I'd like even more than a hand-out?

DAN: That's all I can afford. Business is slow—July's a bad month, people go on vacation.

FEMALE VOICE: Not money. I'd like for you once, just once, to look me in the eye. Eye to eye, like I was a human being. Not garbage.

DAN: Uh. Look. This is getting a little too confrontational for my taste. All I want is to read my paper. You sit down here, you get in my face, you force me to move. Do I deserve that?

FEMALE VOICE: Put the paper down and make eye contact with me.

DAN: I don't have to.

FEMALE VOICE/FERGUS: Dan, get off your high horse and look me in the eye.

DAN: Dan?

FERGUS: Dan. Yes. You're Dan and I'm—

DAN: Fergus, my God. It's you. Jesus H. Christ. You look grotesque.

FERGUS: Thanks.

DAN: The wig and the dress. And the scarf. Sheesh, and the smell. I should've known the smell.

FERGUS: Always an encouraging word.

DAN: Oh, my God. You scared me. What a rotten trick. Sneaking up on me like that. Lipstick and rouge.

FERGUS: It's the sunglasses, see. Otherwise you would've recognized me. It's the sunglasses, they give me a Norma Desmond look.

DAN: And the chest padding. And the falsetto voice. What is this, running around in drag? You look obscene. My God.

FERGUS: Well, I had to do something, Dan. I wasn't scoring. I mean, everyone's being downsized, everyone's short of cash. So first I got a small dog, like I said I would last time we met. A tattered mutt. We were real pathetic together and box office receipts went up. Way up. But Rocky, the mutt, turned on me. I'd buy a sandwich and he'd growl and go for my leg unless I gave it to him. I was lucky if I got three bites. I mean, he knew who the main attraction was. Him. Not me. So I figured, hello, I'm going to end up working for a dog, if this is any indication. Time I broke up the act. So I went to the Goodwill place and got myself a make-over, as they say.

DAN: And people give you money, looking like this?

FERGUS: People don't see the homeless, in case you hadn't noticed. No eye contact. At least not men. They have this vague impression that I'm female. But they don't really look. I just rattle my cup and they pay me to go away. Like you did. It's a nice arrangement, I made eight dollars from Times Square to Coney. Of course I have more overhead this way, make-up is expensive. Maybe it's deductible on my taxes.

P.A. SPEAKER: This is Ocean Parkway. Brighton Beach will be next.

DAN: So where's my coat?

FERGUS: Uh. I better level with you. I swapped it for a good night's sleep. A hotel room. Actually they gave me three nights. It was a good deal. And—while we're at it—where's *my* expensive coat gone?

DAN: It's in my hall closet. Cleaned. Waiting. My mother always asks about it. Why didn't you call? Call collect, if you didn't have the quarter?

FERGUS: I lost your card, and I couldn't remember your last name.

DAN: Listen, I owe you twenty-five bucks. When I got home—imagine how I felt—I found the money in your coat pocket.

FERGUS: *You* felt? Imagine how I felt.

DAN: Let me settle up with you now. Better late than never.

FERGUS: No, it's okay. I've come a long way from where I was six month ago. I've learned that selling your visions for cash is bad Karma.

DAN: But you've gotta live.

FERGUS: Well—

DAN: It's not like you were making a profit. You got paid for your time and effort. Right?

FERGUS: Well, okay.

DAN: Sure. That's the spirit, that's a healthy attitude. I don't have the cash right now, but I'm getting off at Times Square, got a voice-over audition on 46th Street, we can find an ATM.

FERGUS: Uh. Ah—you wouldn't perchance have that flask of Wild Turkey with you, huh?

DAN: That was a one-time thing, that night we met. Just happened I was cleaning out my stuff at Bea's—

FERGUS: Oh, yeah. The girlfriend who wants to be a priest—you still going with her?

DAN: Well. Well, the way it is, we're still together, but we're seeing other people.

FERGUS: Whose lame idea is that?

DAN: Hers, I think. She wants me to, ah, get certain things out of my system— but, of course, soon as I have my freedom, you know how it goes. If you have it, then you don't want it. So I'm, like, killing time.

FERGUS: And your girlfriend, is she seeing anyone?

DAN: She's a pre-priest, Fergus. There's not all that much she can do.

FERGUS: May I ask a favor?

P.A. SPEAKER: Brighton Beach. Watch the closing doors. Sheepshead Bay is next.

DAN: Didn't hear you.

FERGUS: I said, may I ask you a favor?

DAN: You may ask. I might not do it, but you may ask.

FERGUS: Don't call me Fergus, call me Fay.

DAN: Excuse me? Faye—as in Faye Dunaway?

FERGUS: No. Just plain Fay. Eff. A. Why. Fay.

DAN: You're keeping in character, is that it? This gig with the dress and the Shirley Temple curls—it's a method acting exercise, huh? Huuh? Fay?

FERGUS: Ohh. A thrill went through me when you said that. Fay. It's the first time someone besides me has called me Fay.

DAN: Come again.

FERGUS: I mean, you know, Fergus calls me Fay. Of course. But Fergus is part of me, so it hardly counts. You—you, however—because you're on the outside, when you say "Fay," it's a big step forward. You verify my femininity. More than that, you verify my existence.

DAN: Earth to Fergus—yoo-hoo—is anyone there?

FERGUS: Don't spoil it, Dan. Come on, give us a break. It isn't so much to ask. Fay. Say Fay.

DAN: Fay.

FERGUS: Thank you, young man. You're very handsome, you know.

DAN: May-day, May-day. This is not the guy I once knew.

FERGUS: That's right, Fergus is resting. I'm Fay, I'm Fergus's anima. His, well, his female nature. You know about the anima, don't you? Carl Jung and all that? In your case it'd be Danielle, I guess.

DAN: Danielle?

FERGUS: Your friend Fergus broke through to his unconscious (and to me) about three months ago. Listen, let me tell you, I'm very proud of him. Not many people can do that, break through to their animas. He'll tell you it's because he's homeless and starving. He'll say that his withdrawal from the world of material things acted like a prolonged meditation. But it's not as easy as you might think. Poverty can lead to bitterness and despair. It can make the soul clench up. But Fergus stayed open. Almost always. I think you should give him more credit than you do. He could use some praise. Try—next time you see him—try giving Fergus a little positive feed-back.

DAN: Uhh.

P.A. SPEAKER: Sheepshead Bay. Next stop, Neck Road.

DAN: Uhh.

FERGUS: What's wrong? You look sick.

DAN: Oh, I guess that's just how I look in the presence of, of—well, of madness.

FERGUS: Don't be so dismissive.

DAN: Listen—whatever your name is—doesn't all this sound like a major case of schizophrenia? Even to you? What am I supposed to think?

FERGUS: Well, for that matter, what's wrong with schizophrenia?

DAN: All these different personalities—

FERGUS: Aspects of a single personality, Fergus and I are aspects of the Single Being that once was us. In our mother's egg, in the Garden of Eden. Remember, he told you about that.

DAN: Whatever. People with split personalities don't function well in the world.

FERGUS: At this point—what does Fergus have to lose? He's not functioning anyhow. What does Fergus have to lose by accessing his secret feminine nature? Me. By applying his consciousness to the Great Unconscious?

DAN: You mean, uh, that you're the brains behind Fergus?

FERGUS: Oh, he's much smarter than I am. He's a major mind. I'm in the research and collation department, so to speak. My big advantage is, well, I don't sleep, and I don't have to deal with a 3D world, and yes, I've never had to make free will choices. And—what is it?

DAN: Only a friend would tell you, this drag get-up of yours, well, it's gonna set femininity back about ten centuries. It's like you're wearing Frederick's of Calcutta.

FERGUS: This? Come on, Dan. This outfit has nothing to do with me. With me, Fay. You've listened to Fergus, you know the subtle wiring of his mind—he'd never be as obvious as this. This is a costume. An act. In New York you got to give a performance before they shell out any cash.

DAN: So this isn't a sex thing?

FERGUS: Are you implying that there is a *relationship* between Fergus and me—of a reproductive sort? Because I would then advise you to lie down somewhere until that thought goes away.

DAN: Not so loud. People are listening. By sex thing I meant Fergus being a transvestite or something like that. But if you say it's just a *schmatte* to fool the customers with—well, okay.

FERGUS: If Fergus said one thing to you over and over again, it was, try not to think in male-female terms. Use words like Yin and Yang, positive and negative, not "male" and "female." If you use male and female, man and woman, Adam and Eve, then the predictable sexual stereotypes will muscle in. Color. That's an image he gave you. Imagine the color red and the color blue. Mix them together, you get purple. Red isn't better than blue or vice versa. How red and blue make purple is a mystical process. Like the Yin and Yang in the Garden of Eden. In the egg. Remember? That's where I first was separated from him. Where I first came into being.

P.A. SPEAKER: Neck Road. Avenue U coming up.

DAN: Came into being?

FERGUS: In my mother's ovary—as in your mother's ovary—there were many eggs. Each could become a Garden of Eden. Each could contain full potential for Yin and Yang, positive and negative, attraction and repulsion, you name it. But let's go along with the culture and call them Adam and Eve. Just for the moment. Okay?

DAN: You talk as much as Fergus does.

FERGUS: You put me in this position—where I have to explain my existence. The least you can do is listen.

DAN: Fine. Go on. Adam and Eve.

FERGUS: Adam and Eve, but they were one chemical, electrical, magnetic, spiritual—you name it—they made up one *whole*. You couldn't really tell where Eve began and Adam left off. They were like Fergus's example, they were like the vanilla and the fudge of the vanilla fudge ice cream. They were one, they were in love. And, frankly, don't tell anyone, Adam and Eve had no incentive to produce children. Nor did Fergus and I have an incentive. We were sufficient, complete. In some ways we were opposite, but we never opposed one another. It was, well, they call it paradise.

DAN: Are you, for God's sake, gonna get emotional?

FERGUS: No. No. It's just that these things are very available to me now. I can still feel them after more than fifty years.

DAN: Husband and wife.

FERGUS: No, that's the point, it wasn't sexual, reproductive. God gave Eve to Adam as a "help-meet," or so it says in Genesis. And then...

DAN: The sperm, the serpent, the whole shooting match. A sperm came along.

FERGUS: Yes. And it so happened that the sperm contained a Y-chromosome. We call that Y-chromosome the "male" chromosome, but it isn't really. It will help create a male child, but it is really the female aspect of the father, because it couples with Adam and drives Eve into exile. The exquisite peace of the egg is shattered. The female—Eve, me—is exiled to some hidden place in the Garden egg. God allows this—the seduction of Adam by Lilith—because the egg of paradise is too *whole*, too stable. Sterile. Fergus understands this intellectually. I still can *feel* it. The loss. The betrayal I haven't yet forgiven him for. How could he be attracted to *her?* To Lilith—who is known in the Kabala as Adam's mysterious first wife. Who is, in fact, the Y-chromosome. Who brings strange DNA into the egg and forces Eve to become the lost anima. (As an X-chromosome would couple with Eve and force Adam to become the lost animus.) Even now I can recall the full potential of the female and the male living together in an ecstatic joy before the sperm showed up. That's how Jesus could remember His female potential. Experience it. That's how He could die for all of us. For male and female. Because He could remember both genders in the egg—and, by a divine extrapolation, so to speak, He could live out His womanhood.

P.A. SPEAKER: Avenue U. Step carefully. Kings Highway next.

DAN: Right. Jesus died in both genders. You told me that.

FERGUS: I didn't. Fergus did.

DAN: Who's keeping score?

FERGUS: I like to be scrupulous about these matters.

DAN: Why? If you and Fergus were just parts of the same thing?

FERGUS: *Were.* Now it's different. Unlike Fergus, I'm still innocent. I wasn't allowed to make any free will decisions, so my innocence was preserved. Until recently, anyhow.

DAN: Sounds like *Jane Eyre*, the crazy woman in the attic.

FERGUS: I didn't burn the house down, but, yes, I have been crazed. This, what I feel, is the primal loss that we all feel, when we have to choose one gender over another. When—at the command of a stranger—the Yin or Yang is driven out. Sister, brother, gone. Fergus and I had the same DNA, but he still chose Lilith over me. He had me put away. You had Danielle put away.

DAN: I'm not talking until I call my lawyer. Sheesh, I knew it, knew I'd end up taking the rap. I had my anima locked up? Where? Where's the attic?

FERGUS: In the recessive part of the brain—whichever parts those are. In a certain chemical signature that can't express itself. In an electrical charge that is never released. In a ghostlike parallel nervous system that aches like an amputated leg but isn't there. In all those places the lost anima or the lost animus reside.

DAN: The subconscious mind?

FERGUS: No, no, no. The subconscious mind is just a garbage pit, a storage bin for the conscious mind. The unconscious mind, however, is something altogether different. Un-conscious means having no consciousness. Unfortunately we think of sleep when we think of unconsciousness. It isn't as simple as that—to say that "awake" equals conscious and "sleep" equals unconscious. "Unconscious" really means other-than-conscious. A state of being that has no recognizable thoughts or thought processes. The Unconscious is beyond thought, it doesn't have to think. In fact, the Unconscious knows much more than the conscious, because human conscious thought is a very limited way of knowing the Universe of Universes. It's like looking at a palace through a keyhole.

DAN: What other ways of knowing are there?

FERGUS: Many. All of which, you understand, are almost impossible to describe—since description requires language and language requires human consciousness. If you can think about other ways of thinking, then you are no longer thinking, you're doing something else. That's why it's so hard for Fergus and me to communicate. Why it's so hard for you and Danielle. Or hard for Bea and her animus. The animus and the anima live in the Unconscious. If I want to contact Fergus or he wants to contact me, well, then we need some kind of translator. And we need, both of us, to be infinitely open.

P.A. SPEAKER: Kings Highway. Avenue M is next.

DAN: How'd that go again? "If you can think about other ways of thinking—"

FERGUS: —then you are no longer thinking, you're doing something else.

DAN: That sounds like Fergus—so, may I assume the, uh, that the Unconscious Mind is in the brain?

FERGUS: The Unconscious Mind is everywhere. Part of it is in the brain, the part Fergus calls the Autistic Mind. He borrows that term from Joseph Chilton Pearce's book, *The Crack in the Cosmic Egg.* You know it?

DAN: I've seen it in Bea's book case. But no, I don't know it.

FERGUS: In many ways it's an unfortunate term. Autistic. Makes us think of dysfunctional children. Selfishness. Self-absorption. And it is all of those things. May I remind you that I, Fay, his almost mirror image, I was driven into exile. Turned in upon myself. Left with no one I could speak to. Forced to learn another way of thinking—a thoughtless way of thinking.

DAN: A thoughtless way of thinking?

FERGUS: I began to—what? I began to operate, to function, to *be* like the Unconscious Mind. Without thought.

DAN: How?

FERGUS: How? How do you describe Bach to a deaf man? Let me use the conscious mind's terminology. I thought—no. No, I didn't think, I *was* thought continuously. I processed thought without sleeping or ever getting distracted. I processed thought without censorship—censorship by the culture, by the 3D universe, by my own psyche. I took what Fergus saw and felt and imagined and I translated it into the Unconscious Language. But I couldn't see any way of translating it back, into a language that Fergus could understand. And sometimes I was still mad at him. Hurt, not mad.

DAN: An Unconscious pissed-offness.

FERGUS: Of course, all those years, Fergus used me. When he wrote a novel it was me, Fay, that did the metaphor work and thought up the symbols and kept the structure in tune with the themes. Whenever he sat down to write, presto, I was there for him. And he—Mr. Ego—he thought the ideas were coming from his conscious or his subconscious. I could give him the entire plot of a novel, but I couldn't say, "Hello" to him. Where do you think his idea about Jesus dying in both genders came from? Or his idea about the Garden of Eden, about the spear, about Differentness? Huh?

DAN: From you.

FERGUS: I stole them from the Unconscious. Like Prometheus stealing fire. Then I found a way of translating them, of passing them through to his conscious mind.

DAN: I don't get that kind of E-mail.

FERGUS: He was open. I don't minimize that. He took hunger and pain and—what else?—boredom and shame and sorrow. And he turned all those things into a surface noise that distracted his conscious mind. Until the drawbridge came down and let me out. I never thought he'd notice me banging on the pipes upstairs, so to speak. He was such a selfish man. But then it just happened. Of course, it helped that Fergus had a stroke—his dominant male brain shorted out in several of its circuits. It jarred him. He became left-handed. And then one day we began a conversation.

P.A. SPEAKER: Avenue M. Avenue J is next.

FERGUS: It sounded like that. Like that public address speaker's voice—only it was all garbled. Fergus had just given blood at a clinic on West 14th Street and he was shaky as a new-born giraffe. To keep himself from passing out on the L train, he began to interrogate himself. "Does the center of a rotating sphere rotate?' "If God knows everything, can He have ideas?" "Why do men have nipples?" He would ask each question just as his train entered a station—and he would let the electronic gibberish stand as an answer. It was then that I saw my big chance. I began shaping the static. Fergus thought, first off, that he had really gone insane. "Where is the Garden of Eden?" "Livonia Avenue, squawk, in the mother's reproductive tract." "Why does water issue from Jesus's side when the spear enters Him?" "Bushwick Avenue, roar, because Jesus died in childbirth on the cross, breaking His water, bringing forth the new Christian dispensation. Eastern Parkway." For hours Fergus sat on the same train, questioning the electronic voice, afraid to get off. Afraid to lose his place. And finally he asked, "Who are you?" And I said, "Fay. I'm your anima. You don't have to stay on the train, we're together now, Canarsie next."

P.A. SPEAKER: Avenue J. Please don't hold the doors. Avenue H is next.

FERGUS: See?

DAN: So now your mind and Fergus's mind are the same, is that it?

FERGUS: Not the same. But a little of me, a little of the autistic mind, has leaked into him. And a small percent of Fergus has leaked into me. It has altered our velocities. I am not the pure Unconscious any more, I've learned to think. And what a slow, limited Rube Goldberg device that is. Limited and sorrowful. I feel sympathy for you all. And, as for Fergus, well, he's learned about the Universe of Universes—and that's a painful thing to understand.

DAN: The Universe of Universes?

FERGUS: Yes. What Fergus calls his Theophysics. His physics of God. It allowed him to answer, with my help, naturally, the most difficult of all Christian questions. Namely—if God is omniscient and therefore knows the future, how can we have free will? Isn't free will a farce under the circumstances?

DAN: And the answer?

FERGUS: That's a long story.

DAN: You're dicking around with me, Fergus.

FERGUS: Fay.

DAN: Enough with this masquerade. I can't tell you apart, Fay or Fergus. So it makes no sense continuing the impersonation.

FERGUS: He's right, Fay. He's in the physical world, moving with all that high velocity. He doesn't believe that my anima is talking to him. No matter how plausible you sound, he still sees only my busted teeth and the filth on my skin. He doesn't see you in me. He doesn't see how gorgeous you are. And how much you love me. She does, Dan. She's six foot-one. And blonde. With a build on her like Elle MacPherson. I can't exactly see her face, that'd be a mistake, I guess, for me to know exactly what Fay looks like. Too specific. But we've settled on this kind of short-hand to know each other by. In time I'll get more comfortable with the Unconscious and I won't need crutches.

DAN: Uh-huh. Sure.

P.A. SPEAKER: Avenue H. Newkirk next.

DAN: So you started talking to the subway announcements?

FERGUS: I was strung out. I'd lost blood. I was trying to hang onto my consciousness, let alone my sanity. And maybe I chanced upon Fay in the way Jung says he chanced on his anima. By asking questions and listening for an answer. Completing the emotion and waiting for a response. Hearing it. Breathing in and out.

DAN: Where is she now?

FERGUS: She's here.

DAN: Fergus, you're insane. We're sitting on the D train, two dozen people around us, and you're hallucinating. There's no difference between you and Fay.

It's some kind of multiple personality disorder, is all. The Two Faces of Fergus or something.

FERGUS: We differ, Fay and I. Believe me, we differ. It's a matter of velocity. I'm moving as fast as electrons move—and so are you. Fay is almost at rest. In the Unconscious—which, as far as I can tell, is the Mind of God. A place where there is no time. And no speed. And no cause and effect. A place that is both out there and inside.

DAN: Look, my friend. You've got a Grade A brain. You don't need this six-foot bimbo mirage. You can figure it all out by yourself.

FERGUS: Dan. Dan. Don't you think I've already had this argument in my head? Don't you think I've looked down into the pit and seen looniness staring up at me? But finally I couldn't deny her. Not just because she was beautiful and she loved me. But because she answered all the questions. And there was an elegance to her thinking that appealed to me.

P.A. SPEAKER: This is Newkirk Avenue. Cortelyou next.

FERGUS: Like the problem of God's omniscience and our free will. What she was talking about just a minute ago, before I came back. That was, from my childhood, an annoying riddle. If God already knows the free will choices I will make—well, what's the sense in going through the motions? It's all a charade. Or so it would seem. Right?

DAN: Right. Sure. You bet.

FERGUS: It stumped me. There I was on the train, talking to what I thought was this scrambled subway intercom, and—among other things—I ask about, you know, how God can be omniscient and still claim we have free will, and she says, Fay says—get this—"Because God and the Great Universe of Universes are just a single instant, just one single event." And, blammo, I understood.

DAN: I'm glad you do.

FERGUS: Think about it. Never mind what you and I perceive about time, let's say that there is *only one moment.* Everything—creation, continuance, finish, infinity—everything is contained in a single moment of no-time. Moment is, in fact, a misleading word because it implies a moment before or after, a series of things that we call the passage of time. But God is the eternal instant. How's that for an oxymoron? He is the Once that goes on forever. So, if there is only this single instant, then God's omniscience and your act of free will, they occur at the same moment of no-time. They occur simultaneously. They are both immediate.

DAN: Hmmm.

FERGUS: Time, you see, is a pernicious concept—a concept we need to be liberated from. Get rid of time and what else goes? Well, for one, all ideas of speed disappear. Velocity—miles per hour—velocity is a function of time. In the Eternal Instant, therefore, you have no speed. Nor is space relevant: if everything exists in the Eternal Instant, then everything is where it always has been and always will be. There are no destinations, nor any starting points. Better yet, without time, there can be no cause and effect. Cause supposes a state of affairs that is prior. Effect supposes a state of affairs that is after. Without before and after there can be no cause and effect. Imagine: no cause and no effect.

DAN: Seems to me there's not much left. You've kinda reasoned yourself out of business.

FERGUS: It's all still there. All we've done is get rid of some ideas that depend on relationships. Like time and speed. Cause and effect.

DAN: Well, if I figure this right—uhhh—without cause and effect you can't have any good or any bad. No morality.

FERGUS: It's all still there. We've lost nothing. I'm just describing it differently. I now use simple algebra. Take an electric lamp. You press the switch and it goes on. Letter A—your finger pressing the switch—leads to letter B, a lighted lamp. In our present state of consciousness you would say that A leads to B. But in the Eternal Instant you express it as AB. The dark lamp and the lit lamp exist together. So do C D E F G H I and J as the light goes off and on, off and on, off and on. They all exist in the one instant.

DAN: I'm having a little trouble visualizing this.

FERGUS: Okay, I have a useful analogy for you.

P.A. SPEAKER: Cortelyou Road. We have a red signal against us. Thanks for your patience, we will be moving shortly. Beverley Road is next.

FERGUS: Damn.

DAN: What's wrong?

FERGUS: Got to take a leak. Can't afford any more red signals. Analogy, yes. I have a useful analogy.

DAN: Relax. Don't feel you've gotta give me a lecture—

FERGUS: Indulge me. Keeps my mind off my bladder, which feels like an inflated blowfish right now. So, so—so, a useful analogy. Take a movie projector.

DAN: Yes?

FERGUS: Frames of film pass in front of a powerful light and—by so doing— they give the impression of motion on a screen. Two lovers kiss. One cowboy shoots another cowboy. People move and are moved. That's why they call them movies or motion pictures. Correct?

DAN: You're leading to something.

FERGUS: Right. Because it's an illusion, as we know. The movement that makes a movie—it doesn't occur on screen. It occurs instead at a very different place—at the projector. Where frames, just so many still photographs, pass at great speed in front of the light. Giving the illusion of movement on a screen. So—

DAN: Go on.

FERGUS: But it's still an illusion. We know that much. We know that the lovers haven't really kissed. We are looking at life in a purely artificial way. A play of light and lenses. In any given year we spend hundreds of hours watching the photographic ghosts of people as they move across a screen. And yet, when we leave the theatre we somehow accept the cars and buildings outside, accept them as being *real*. We don't question them. Do you question the fact that we are talking right now in a stopped D train

DAN: No. Should I?

FERGUS: Probably. Wise men throughout time have concerned themselves with illusion and reality. Plato's cave in *The Republic*, what is it but a movie theatre? Remarkable prescience on Plato's part in 400 b.c. or so. To foretell the invention of projectors and screens. You remember Plato's cave?

DAN: Uh. Haven't read it since Columbia.

FERGUS: People are chained from birth in what you'd call the orchestra section. They can't leave and they can only look in one direction, at the screen. On this screen shadows are cast. The viewers think the shadows are real because, after all, they've been in the cave all their lives—they have nothing else to compare the cave experience with. Actually, though, the shadows are caused by a kind of puppet show. Puppeteers are pushing statues and trees and whatever in front of a big bonfire. Behind the chained watchers. The bonfire acts exactly as the projector in a modern movie theatre acts. It's an amazing bit of prophecy.

DAN: Yes. Comes back to me now.

FERGUS: Plato describes what would happen to a man who was allowed to leave the cave. He would see the real world—real trees and people. He would know the difference between shadow and substance. But no one in the cave would believe him—try as he might to tell them about reality. They just wouldn't have the concepts and categories necessary to understanding.

P.A. SPEAKER: We're still under a red signal. Thanks for your patience.

FERGUS: But let's take Plato and update him a bit. He didn't know, after all, about frames and slo-mo and flashbacks. Let's imagine that each frame of a film represents an instant of time. A given, basic unit of time. We see the film (we see life) as a series of instants, one after another. Frame A then B then C then D. Played at such a speed that A, slightly different from B, will meld with B and give the illusion of time and speed and cause and effect. But there is another way to see those frames.

DAN: I'm supposed to ask how. How?

FERGUS: You can see the frames as God sees them. Not one by one by one in serial fashion. God, remember, is a single instant. So, imagine this. God takes the film that is your life and He snips between the frames. He makes a pile of frames. He stacks them up in one very tall pile. And then with the projection light of ten billion God-watts, He sees the entire film in a single instant. Flash.

DAN: He sees everything at the same time? Same moment?

FERGUS: Yes. The series of instants that were frame A and B and C and D have become ABCD. With a powerful enough light you can see the entire stack of frames as one frame. It makes for a complex and busy moment. But this is God we're talking about. He has a high IQ. When He sees the entire stack of frames projected on the screen in one instant, well, He takes that One picture and deduces a lifetime from it. An eternity, in fact. It's the difference between seeing something head-on or side-on. Seeing it as points or as waves. Ah, we're moving.

DAN: But God doesn't. He doesn't move, right? If everything occurs in one moment, then—then God is just sitting there.

FERGUS: That's what it looks like to us. We who once thought the sun went around the earth. But movement itself is an illusion. Like one cowboy shooting another cowboy on the screen. It doesn't really happen. So—to say that God sits there—that's a judgment forced on us by our own false sense of movement. God is stillness. The great contemplative monks knew this: the way to spirituality is along the path of no-movement. Motionless Oneness. God seeks to be at rest in the Eternal Instant that is no-time. The one instant that holds all instants. The one instant that's perfect. Almost.

DAN: Did you say *almost*?

P.A. SPEAKER: Beverley Road. Next stop Church Avenue.

DAN: God is almost what?

FERGUS: Almost perfect.

DAN: Is that heresy or something? I hear tell that God is perfect.

FERGUS: He is. In fact His imperfection makes Him perfect.

DAN: This is hard.

FERGUS: Don't fade out on me now. Remember what I told you that night in January when first we met. God is love, we accept that. But if God were alone, then he would have nothing but Himself to love. And such love we call narcissism. And God cannot be narcissistic, so He must create something—something other than Himself to love. Some intelligent other being with free will. Some being different from God. Since God is stillness, this different other being must have some motion. And, because there must be motion, God's universe is not fully at rest. In that sense He is not perfect. God's one imperfection is His love. Love is a transitive verb, remember I told you that. Instead of settling into perfect, self-satisfying stillness, God must heal, forgive, console, adore the beings that He has created. God is love in motion. The first principle of Fergus Quirk's Theophysics.

DAN: I think I've got it. Let me go over this in my head a moment. Uh, yes. Yes, okay.

FERGUS: Because—

DAN: Wait.

P.A. SPEAKER: Church Avenue, Parkside next.

DAN: So I have time and speed, but God doesn't have time and speed.

FERGUS: It's simple. Let me do it again. For God to love us we must be something different from Him. God is perfect stillness therefore we—to be different—we must move (or think we move). God is one instant, therefore we—to be different—must exist (or think we exist) in more than one instant. These concepts—movement, time—are all illusions, as I said. We're all still contained in the One Eternal Instant of God. But illusions can be powerful, everyone knows that. We are the people who are born, live and die in Plato's cave. We invented the cinema and we invented virtual reality. Who's to say God can't invent us—then just set us moving at the correct projection speed?

DAN: It's complicated.

FERGUS: Complicated? It's child's play, if you ask me. Certainly child's play compared to what they ask us to believe about the computer universe. Tell me, for instance, where a web site is. Go on, tell me.

DAN: Where a web site is?

FERGUS: Yes. Before you call it up on your computer screen. After you click it off. Where does it live? Where? They call it a site, where is it situated?

DAN: Oh, I'm not the one to ask. I'm still in the age of steam.

FERGUS: Far as I can see, the Theophysical Universe is much easier to comprehend. Maybe we were all created as web sites by God's lap top machine.

P.A. SPEAKER: This is Parkside. This train will not stop at Prospect Park. Seventh Avenue is next.

FERGUS: So God's great gift to us—it's His willingness to exist in time and speed for our sakes. God's tendency is to seek stillness, but—because we are His creatures and because He loves us—God takes on our nature. Jesus is not just born into the flesh, incarnated, He is also born into time and speed and cause and effect. And, believe me, that great sacrifice is enough to heal the entire Universe of Universes.

114

DAN: Why do you call it that?

FERGUS: It's logical enough. To repeat: God is love. God must give love—transitive verb—God must give love to everything intelligent that's different from Him. God is stillness, so we know that Differentness is characterized by at least some amount of time and speed. For every possible time/speed there is a different universe. Since there are an infinite number of time/speeds, there are an infinite number of universes. Hence Universe of Universes.

DAN: So ours is not the only universe?

FERGUS: There is a separate—and very different—universe for every expression of time/speed.

DAN: Like light-years, you mean?

FERGUS: Not necessarily. There are universes, I presume, that do not even register light. It always makes me sad, when some astronomer or professor of physics delivers himself of a new Big Bang theory. Our scientific understanding—such as it is—applies to just this single universe out of an infinity of universes. If the motion of our universe is given arbitrarily as five time/speeds, then there is also a complete and infinite universe at 4.999999 t/s and at 5.00001 t/s. And so on.

DAN: God must create a universe for every different rate of time and speed?

FERGUS: It's not easy being Him. He's omniscient, remember. More than that, as Saint Isaac of Nineveh said fourteen hundred years ago, "All that the Lord thinks, He does." It must be a hassle. Whatever God thinks about—that image or idea at once becomes reality. It *is*. It comes into being. It takes effect.

P.A. SPEAKER: Seventh Avenue. Atlantic Avenue will be next.

DAN: I'm not sure I understand what you mean by time/speed.

FERGUS: Well, for a moment, let's go back to my frame analogy again. God is a single frame, a single instant of no-time, no-speed. Right?

DAN: Right. I think.

FERGUS: What then would be the first universe, so to speak? The first universe that God would create? (I'm using this as a rhetorical device, of course. God created all universes at the same instant.) But if He created the Universe of Universes in order of size, what would come first? Logically.

DAN: You got me.

FERGUS: Well, obviously, it would be a universe made up to *two* frames. At two frames things begin to change. There is time, there is speed. Frame two seems to follow from frame one. There appears to be cause and effect. All our troubles begin—or seem to begin—when God allows the second frame to exist. Because He must love. And because He must love something different from Himself. Which a second frame would be.

DAN: Okay. And by time/speed you mean what?

FERGUS: It's an imaginary unit: one that expresses a certain relationship between time and speed—and then uses that relationship, in turn, to express some composite yet single time/speed velocity. A joint rate, you might say. Metaphorically speaking, time/speed corresponds to the amplitude and frequency of a wave. That's what a universe is—it's a wave traveling at a certain t/s. In fact, to remind myself of that, I prefer to call it a wave-universe.

P.A. SPEAKER: Atlantic Avenue. This is a Manhattan-bound D train. Dekalb Avenue next.

DAN: So where we exist now is—uh… give me a hint.

FERGUS: We live in a wave-universe that is the material expression of a certain time/speed. We *are* that time/speed. We characterize it. We give it soul. It is this wave universe that best expresses our peculiar genius and temperament. Though, due to a perverse will, we too often act against the nature and the innate rhythms of that wave universe.

DAN: It's poetical. But hard to accept.

FERGUS: I don't know why. I mean, you turn on the TV and there's Dan Rather doing the news. Right? Then you flip the channel and you're watching a cartoon show. Surf some more and you get *Star Trek* or Yankee baseball or whatever. Right? Each seems to be a separate world. Yet those worlds are, in fact, just the product of certain waves being transmitted through the ether. They're pretty damned convincing, wouldn't you say? And, and, and—what'll happen when the virtual reality machines become commonplace? The technological culture—since Plato's cave—has been undermining our smug assumptions about reality and illusion. The truth is: reality and illusion are beginning to merge. Certainly—at the level of sub-atomic particles, anyway—there is very little difference between the real and the unreal. What happens when we become totally computer-bound and out of touch with the 3D "real" world? What happens when the 2D image on your computer screen becomes the superior reality? Because it is the more familiar reality? Gradually we're being conditioned to live without reality. To see through, then dismantle, our 3D habits. To exist in the empty space between the atoms. To stop playing our particular movie frame by frame in time and at a given speed. To play it, instead, as God plays it. In one frame. Always here and now. In the moment which is all moments. Uhhh-wow.

DAN: What?

FERGUS: Gotta hit the porcelain. Real bad.

P.A. SPEAKER: Dekalb Avenue. Grand Street is next.

FERGUS: Uhhh.

DAN: Be brave.

FERGUS: At my age you don't show disrespect to your bladder. Uhh. All my drainage equipment could go—snappo—just like that.

DAN: Look. We're over the river. That'll take your mind off things. It's gotten hazy out.

FERGUS: Uhh.

DAN: Remember, last time we were here, you were talking about Differentness. Since then all I've heard about is cloning. How does cloning factor in?

FERGUS: Uhh.

DAN: Fergus?

FERGUS: It's not Fergus, it's Fay.

DAN: Fay? Fay again. Why can't I just speak to Fergus?

FERGUS: His conscious mind couldn't stand the pain any more. He is, while we speak, he's in deep bladder denial. So I get to drive. As for cloning, I have mixed feelings about it. Yes, there is too much Differentness and strife. And sexual reproduction increases that. Males compete—socially, fiscally, biologically—they compete for the right to fertilize as many female ova as they can. Even in the race to the womb, as early as that, sperm attack and repel one another. It is innate. Struggle. War. One punch street fights in the parking lot outside a bar. But there is no competition when you clone. No elbowing between the male sperm as they swim upstream. No trauma, no Fall of Man, as there is now, when a sperm comes hurtling in to fertilize the Garden of Eden egg. There's a lot to be said for it, cloning. They use an ordinary cell in cloning. Cloning doesn't require an X or Y reproductive cell to jump start the process. Just any old cell—a piece of leg, a piece of tongue. No romance, no sentiment. Yes, you can make an argument for cloning. But then—

P.A. SPEAKER: Grand Street. Let them off. Next stop Broadway-Lafayette.

DAN: But then?

FERGUS: I am a child of sexual reproduction. If there is no so-called Fall of Man, if the sperm doesn't enter the egg either as a male or a female interloper, then—well, then there is no tension between male and female, Yin and Yang, Adam and Eve. I am not driven into exile.

DAN: That's bad?

FERGUS: In many ways. If Eve is not driven out—then she and Adam live in innocence together. The sperm does not fertilize, the egg just splits. The apple is not eaten. Adam and Eve do not know Differentness and the mortality that comes with it. They're, well, bland. Because Eve has not been driven out into the autistic mind—because of that, she cannot establish contact with God's Unconscious. What has happened to Fergus through me—his breaking into the Unconscious—could not happen to the cloned male or the cloned female. They are limited by their love. By their Oneness. By their dreary artificial garden.

DAN: Always a catch to it someplace.

FERGUS: There is no understanding without a sense of loss.

DAN: I don't feel any of this, Fergus. Uh, Fay. I don't have that sense of loss. It doesn't ring a bell with me. Call me insensitive or whatever.

FERGUS: It takes time. It took Fergus 56 years and a major stroke before he slowed down enough. Slowed enough so that he could approach moments of utter stillness. Or I could reach his speed. This is a very fast wave-universe that we live in. The faster things go, the more "real" they seem. The more physical reality they seem to have. As you go slower, well, the more they appear to lose momentum. The more they tend to disintegrate. As a two-wheel bicycle falls over when the pedaling stops. It's scary. Where I live—in the autistic mind—the mind that is innocent because it has made no free will choices—where I live the autistic mind is almost at stillness. Almost at God speed. In all of us. If we can slow down enough.

P.A. SPEAKER: Broadway-Lafayette. Let them off. West 4th Street next.

FERGUS: Listen, Dan. I'm getting off at West 4th street. I know where there's a john at West 4th.

DAN: No. Come with me to 42nd and Sixth.

FERGUS: I can't. Can't. I let things go too far. This is serious business I'm in now.

DAN: But your money? How'll you get your money? All I have on me now is two quarters and a token. Look, stay on 'til we get to 42nd and Sixth. There has to be a public lavatory at 42nd and Sixth. I've got a quick voice-over audition. Ten minutes at most. Then I'll run over to my ATM and get some cash. Then we'll find a quiet place for lunch. Anyway, I wanna talk with you about, you know, maybe writing some of this stuff down.

FERGUS: Thanks. Thanks. But let me take a rain check on that. It's a long ride to 42nd.

DAN: You'll call me? I'm in the Brooklyn book. Daniel Rusher. Call collect.

FERGUS: I will.

DAN: No. You won't call. I know you won't call.

FERGUS: Sure, I will.

DAN: No, you won't. Okay, see what: I'll get off at West 4th Street with you. Then I'll call my agent and say I'm in a horrendous subway jam. Maybe they'll put my audition back an hour or so.

FERGUS: You don't have to do that.

DAN: I want to. What's another audition anyway? And besides, I just figured, if I'm gonna be seen walking with a derelict in drag, then I'd rather be seen on West 4th street than on 42nd. You have a downtown look.

FERGUS: Do you *really* think so?

DAN: Who am I talking to?

FERGUS: Us.

DAN: And why not? Who's to say Fay doesn't exist? Who's to say we're not just some bunch of images projected on a screen? Hey, it's a free country.

FERGUS: Right now I'm trying to keep my socks from bubbling. Uhhh. The 3D universe has really gotten my attention. Here we are, praise God. It's crowded. Lucky for me, people don't tend to stand in my way.

P.A. SPEAKER: This is West 4th Street.

FERGUS: Upstairs and to the right.

DAN: Excuse us, excuse us.

FERGUS: No, this is the mezzanine. One more flight. Owww—I don't think I'll make it.

DAN: You will.

FERGUS: Down this way, to the toll booth. Uh.

DAN: Where? Oh, yes. Here's the MENS room. I'll wait outside and make a call to my agent.

FERGUS: Okay.

DAN: Wait, Fergus. Stop! That's the LADIES room. Wait! Damn. Now what's he done? Oh, man. That idiot. He went into the LADIES room. Phone. Yes, hello—Rita? This is Dan Rusher. I'm out on a call—I need to speak with Jeb. He isn't? Well, look I'm in a jam. Yes, I'm at a public phone. 673-3447. Would you? It's 3:15. I'll stay here until 3:25. 673-3447. Just a second—Miss! Miss! I wouldn't use that bathroom. There's—uh—a leak.

LADY ONE: A leak?

DAN: One of the facilities backed up. You'll ruin your shoes.

LADY ONE: Well, thank you.

DAN: Hello, Jeb. That's all right. I took sick in the train. I'm down at West 4th Street recovering. No, I'm fine. One of those twenty-four hour things. But I'm going to miss the Union Bank audition at O'Leary and Mantell. Could you smooth it over with them? I would myself—except I forgot the casting lady's name. Thanks. No, don't change any bookings for tomorrow. Okay—what time is it now? 3:30? Have I been here fifteen minutes. Let me run. Miss! Miss!

LADY TWO: Yes.

DAN: Excuse me. But a friend of mine just went into the LADIES. I mean, uh—she fell sick and went in there fifteen minutes ago. Will you check and see if she's all right? I'm a little shy about looking in there. If you don't mind.

LADY TWO: Sure. What's her name?

DAN: Fay. She—ah, she over-dresses a little.

LADY TWO: I'll be right out.

DAN : Jesus, Dan. You did the wrong thing. In a minute she'll come out of there screaming bloody murder. Cops'll haul Fergus away. Uh-oh.

LADY TWO: There's no Fay in there. Fact is—there's no nobody in there. You seemta lost your girlfriend, mister.

DAN: How can that be? I've been standing right here, by the phone, with my eye on the door. The whole time. Are you sure?

LADY TWO: There ain't but two stalls in there all told. You sure maybe she went in the MENS room by mistake?

DAN: Could it be? No. I saw him go through that door on the left.

LADY TWO: Him?

DAN: Her, I mean.

LADY TWO: Mister—you better look in the MENS I think you ain't seein so good.

DAN: I will. Thanks for your trouble. I'll go in now. Fergus! Yo, Fergus.

MAN: What's up, Dude?

DAN: Oh, have you been in here all this while?

MAN: What's that to you? If I wanna comb my hair just right? If you from the police, you lookin' in the wrong place. I's not holdin' nothing. I'm clean.

DAN: No, I'm not the police. I'm looking for a friend. He came in here twenty minutes ago, I think.

MAN: Nobody here but me. Since I come in, and I been here since three o'clock..

DAN: How can that be? Is there anyone in the stall?

MAN: They's nothing in there 'cept a skanky old blonde wig someone left. See? And a dress.

DAN: Ah.

MAN: Hey, Dude, you don't look so good. You look white like somebody just died.

DAN: Ah.

MAN: Hold my hand, man. Hold my hand. You gonna fall down.

PART THREE

SEX AND CANNIBALISM

[*It was around one p.m. on a Wednesday, seven months later, that I ran into Fergus again. I had just knocked down a vodka tonic at Hogs and Heifers—a pretty dismal experience, believe me. I mean, at Hogs and Heifers, if you don't need a stiff one before you come into the joint, you need one after. The place is like a cheap museum—with its silly wallfull of discarded and grimy old brassieres, artifacts of some forgotten genderal war. Fingers of black soot radiate out from the ceiling fan motor. At night, with the Drew Barrymore types there, I'm told, Hogs and Heifers is, um, authentic or something. With just me and the bar girl there at midday or so, it was like taking an old wooden freight elevator to the basement of nowhere.*

I was anyway disgusted with life. A male friend had stood me up. The March wind outside was full of hacksaw blades. I had given a lousy audition for Jamie in Long Day's Journey *at the Hudson River Rep (that's why I had the tape recorder with me). My income derived almost* in toto *from a voice-over I'd done for some hemorrhoid preparation eight months before. Not that I was being elitist or anything. It just didn't make me feel, oh, well, serious.*

Plus I had spent ten weeks getting my dead mother's estate in order. What a paper trail that was. She kept no records—except for an intimate diary that I was too scared to read. Suddenly, with Mom out of the house, there was no reason for me and my fiancée not to marry and move in together—either at her place or at mine. So, of course, Bea and I panicked. She came down with shingles and couldn't be touched. I sprained my back. And there was something about my mother's painful dying—the horrible rack she was on—that made me feel rebellious in church. I saw Jesus hanged on His cross and all at once my sullen feet refused to approach the communion rail. I guess I simply didn't feel

126

like being an accomplice in so much misery. It was just a stage, I suppose. I was withholding from God. Bea, however, took it as a betrayal of our relationship (she was, after all, going to be ordained and had, therefore, a stake in my conformity). And maybe my mother's death affected me more than I was willing to let on about.

Ice and wind strafed me when I pushed out onto Washington Street. The West Side Meat Market, what's left of it, is a discouraging sight. At that time of day the roofed-over loading docks—rickety with age, sodden with old blood—are unoccupied. Carcasses will not hang from the sliding meat racks again until tomorrow morning. Even at 20 degrees F. a sweet stench of massacred flesh breathes in and out: you could make gravy from it.

And there, standing calf-deep in a Dumpster, was Fergus Quirk.

Not that I recognized him at first. In fact I walked past the Dumpster, did a double-take and came back. Fergus had grown a full (and bird-dung colored) beard. Now both upper front teeth were missing (his tongue tip tends to push out through the tooth gap when his jaw as at rest). Each crack and pucker in Fergus's skin had been lined with charcoal pencilings of filth. And, on his vein-shot nose, there was this growth like a potato's eye. A little sea cucumber.

But I remembered the woolen JETS hat—and the uneven gait brought on by his stroke (his shoulders swiveled and shrugged to take some responsibility away from his gimpy right foot). His hands were wearing crusty Ace bandages, like a boxer's, taped. Animal fat and gristle stuck to Fergus's corduroy pants legs. In his left hand there was the pink-white shin bone of a steer. He jabbed and lifted with it. He dug a trench in the butcher mess. And, when I got close, I caught his peculiar smell.

"Fergus," I said. (I had to shout: the wind got noisy then, and Fergus was preoccupied with his rooting around. I didn't like to watch it.) "Fergus. It's me. It's Dan."

"Uh," he said. "Uh-uh. You."

"Dan Rusher—don't you remember me?"

"Dan."

"What in God's name are you doing?"

"What? I'm starved out of my mind is what. Don't give me no high and mighty attitudes." He put the bone against his lips—more to gross me out than to bite nourishment off. (There were only strings of sinew on it, and his teeth were frail.)

"Stop it," I said. *"Get out of that thing."*

"There's nothing wrong with this. It's fresh. There's no law says I can't eat it. I eat here all the time."

"Fergus. Don't get in a pride place. Climb out and let me buy you a meal."

"I've eaten worse than this."

"I'm sure you have. But let's go over to the diner, to Peronista's. Let's have a meal. I'm freezing."

"I don't think I can get out."

"Yes, you can. Sure, you can."

"Lean over and give me a yank." I—well, of course I hesitated. The bandages on his hands were wet with what looked like suet. Yet I didn't want to insult him by putting my gloves on. *"If it's not too much trouble."*

"What is this, Fergus—a test?"

"I can't get out. I'm standing on meat—give me your hand."

"All right, all right."

"Pull hard."

"I am."

"Hard."

128

His feet came out of the animal mulch with a sucking burp. Fergus balanced on the Dumpster rim for five or six uncertain beats, then he fell to the pavement—first making sure he brushed against my new overcoat. There was always some slapstick in his desperation. But, despite the cold, Fergus had a malarial glaze of sweat on his neck and forehead. And when I held the door to Peronista's open for him, I saw, on close inspection, a yellow, yolk-like material in each eye.

Note: the place, thank God, was empty and unpretentious. We sat in a dim booth near the MENS. At that moment, hanging up my coat, I remembered the tape machine (it was in my pocket). After the two previous meetings with Fergus I have had to depend entirely on recall. What follows here is a verbatim transcript of the conversation between us. I have interjected marginalia, as it were, to explain events and to indicate (where appropriate) the state of my mind.]

WAITER: Menus?

FERGUS: Give me five burgers—

DAN: Fergus—

FERGUS: Five burgers, no fries. And a salami on roll to start.

DAN: Are you sure that's good for you?

FERGUS: I'm sure that's good for me.

WAITER: How would you like the meat done?

FERGUS: Yesterday. Quickly. It doesn't matter. I can't taste anyway. Taste is for rich people.

WAITER: To drink—ah—sir?

FERGUS: Beer. Not lite. Real beer.

DAN: Iced tea. For now. Can I smoke?

WAITER : I wish you would. I'll be right back.

FERGUS: I wish you would? What does that mean?

DAN: You know what it means. Hey—don't eat the catsup like that. Don't give him a reason to break our chops. For God's sake Fergus, you smell awful and you look awful. I tell people I met this scuzzy guy in the subway—and I romanticize it. I forget how really messed up you are. What happened to your other tooth?

FERGUS: It just gave up. Fell apart. Like a sugar cube.

DAN: It looks like you have a fever.

FERGUS Phlebitis in my leg. Flu. Gum abscess. Some kind of foot rot. Whatever.

DAN: Why didn't you call me?

FERGUS: Ho, sure.

DAN: I gave you my number.

FERGUS: Ho, sure.

WAITER: Salami. Beer. Iced Tea.

DAN: That's not fair. I would've helped. I typed out all the stuff you told me. Both times. I've given it to friends. I wanted to talk things over with you. I *wanted* you to call me.

FERGUS: Okay, whatever. I'm sorry I underestimated you. I should have called. Pardon my lack of self-worth. Let me eat.

DAN: Listen. You're in this downward spiral. You're wallowing in it. You're gonna pick up a septic condition and just die.

FERGUS: I have some antibiotics. I'll go to St. Vincent's and they'll give me a refill.

DAN: This isn't a matter of antibiotics. You're totally run down. From the color in your eyes, there's some kind of hepatitis I bet. Or cirrhosis. You need a rest. Regular food. New clothes.

130

FERGUS: What—

WAITER: First burger.

FERGUS: Thanks. Nother beer. What—so what are you proposing?

DAN: Come on out to Coney Island and live with me. Do it. Accept a gift.

FERGUS: Live with you? Uh-huh. Your mother would just love that.

DAN: My mother is dead. She died three months ago.

FERGUS: Mm. Sorry.

DAN: So you can have her room. Got a view of the ocean. We'll work on a book. I consider it an investment.

FERGUS: That's very good of you. I'll think about it.

DAN: What's to think about? You're not gonna get a better offer. Not today, not this afternoon.

FERGUS: What about this girlfriend of yours, aren't you getting married?

DAN: Bea has her own place. She won't mind. Anyway, we're working things out. Right now.

FERGUS: That doesn't sound good.

DAN: It's okay. These things happen. What with my mother's death and all, we haven't been too intimate. And so forth. You know. Besides, I'm having trouble with the Christian thing. The crucifixion, the Mass. And that bugs her.

FERGUS: Problem is—you wanted to eat them both.

DAN: What?

FERGUS: You wanted to eat them both, your mother and the girlfriend.

DAN: Eat them? Are you delirious?

WAITER: Burger number two.

FERGUS: Keep them coming. Nother beer. My friend's good for it.

WAITER: And you sir?

DAN: I'm fine.

FERGUS: Get him a little female flesh.

WAITER: Excuse me?

FERGUS: Nothing. It's the beer talking.

WAITER: I'll bring your next burger.

DAN: What's with you now? Have you gone totally insane?

FERGUS: Dan, baby. I've had a vision.

DAN: What else is new?

FERGUS: Right out of the Collective Unconscious. A vision like Ringling Brothers—a circus of the psyche. Not to mention the side show. And, you—gerp. Pardon me. *You* can have the same vision. Yes, unimaginative, matter-of-fact, you. You can see the truth.

DAN: Keep your voice down.

FERGUS: Because I, Fergus, have found a pure meditative state. Better than TM or Yoga or whatever your favorite drug is. Do you want to know what it is?

DAN: Listen, you don't have to perform for your supper. Relax. We can talk tomorrow. Just eat.

[At that moment, if I remember right, I probably didn't want to hear about Fergus's new vision. His few references to female flesh had spooked me enough. I was, anyhow, superstitious about Fergus. (And, it's true, I had a stake in him. If he wasn't wise etc., what was I doing with this homeless tramp? My friends asked me that.) But I couldn't play hard-to-get with Fergus. He was becoming hyper at this point—exhilaration from beer and meat. I wanted to calm him down. And besides—I couldn't hide it—Fergus knew my tape recorder was on. He knew I was interested.]

FERGUS: Yo, wake up. You wanna know what the perfect meditative state is? Or not?

DAN: So what's the perfect meditative state?

FERGUS: Starvation. I have seen it. Yes. Fun? No, I didn't say it was fun. It's like your guts start to calcify. Then there's this ringing in your ears— not music, just one or two long notes. Like the noise they put on with a TV test pattern. But it can get, like, operatic, the way monotonous things do. Feverish. Brrrr-brrr-brrr. That's the sound of death pouring in. Brrrr-rrrr-brrrrr. Your head is detached from your body. What use is your body? You can hardly move it. It's no good even as a food storage locker any more. You have tuned in on the primal harmony. Last month, in my already wretched state, I got locked in at the place where I was living. I ended up going four days without solid food.

DAN: Jesus.

FERGUS: Oh, the death song was being sung. Brrrrrrrrr. And I was screening some pretty gruesome hallucinations, you betcha.

DAN: I imagine.

FERGUS: Don't kid yourself, you don't. You don't imagine. But I said to myself, when I was sane—which was at least some of the time—I said, "Fergus, you're like one of those desert saints. No food. No desire. Blind in the dark. You're a little ball of consciousness with no prejudices left, just hanging out where the black holes live. Why don't you ask some questions? This is the time for eternal truth." I sincerely didn't care whether I lived or died.

WAITER: Burger number three.

DAN: Fergus—

FERGUS: It's not for your sake. Not particularly. It's for my sake. I need to talk.

DAN: All right.

FERGUS: So, anyway, I wanted to ask a question. About God, should I ask about God? No. I was scared to do that: it seemed, you know, a little presumptuous. So I asked about man. What is man? And it came to me, along with the locusts buzzing in my ear. It came to me that you can safely say one thing about all men and all women. One thing.

DAN: And I'm supposed to ask what? What?

FERGUS: They're hungry. Men and women are hungry almost all the time.

DAN: Fergus. Under the circumstances—don't you think that's kinda predictable? You were starving. What else is your mind gonna say? Give me a break.

FERGUS: But I was dying. If EMS hadn't come, I would've died. I was almost not-hungry for the first time, I was almost dead. The big thing about death is— you don't need to eat any more. Listen, I'm not talking about the soul. I'm not talking about man's capacity to love God. I'm talking about that animal we live with. Between that animal and any other animal in the world you can be sure of one thing—they're both hungry.

DAN: So. That's not news.

FERGUS: Yeah, but we try to forget about it. Everything we do—work, play, sleep—it's all to distract us from eating. You know what a massive job it is to keep just one human digestive system going? How big's the burger I've been eating, say? Say, six square inches. If I eat just one a day for sixty years, how much meat do I need? I did the math in my head last night. About 130,000 square inches of hamburger, that's what. A four-story building filled with burgers. And who eats just one a day? You and I could fill a whole neighborhood with the food we put away in a lifetime.

WAITER: Number four.

DAN: Right on cue.

FERGUS: And coffee.

DAN: I need a coffee, too. No cream.

FERGUS: And there's so many of us. Where has the food been coming from? Work, play, sleep—it's all to distract us, so we don't eat up the whole world by mistake some day.

DAN: You don't mention sex.

FERGUS: Aha. But you knew it was coming. Eventually you knew I'd get around to it, to sex. Hold that thought until I come back from the john. My sweetbreads are in an uproar. Ahem.

[*Tape 1A ran out here.*]

DAN: Testing: one, two, three. Oh. Fergus. You're back. You all right?

FERGUS: It'll do, it'll do. Where were we?

DAN: I don't know, a vision, something.

FERGUS: Right, okay. Pass the sugar and pay attention. I'm about to deliver myself of a few home truths.

DAN: Uh-oh.

FERGUS: So, listen. Just after life came into being—long before love, long even before sex—death came into being. The need to kill and the fear of being killed. The need to eat and the fear of being eaten. Believe me, Dan boy, sexual reproduction, lust, is not the essential human urge—though Freud wanted us all to think so. The essential human urge is to eat. People who are malnourished can't get erections, tell me about it. People who are starving don't have periods. You can do without sex—even if it means the species will die out. You can't do without eating. And soon. No, not soon. Now.

DAN: But—

FERGUS: Sssh, I'm on a riff. Why d'you think sex is so far-out exquisite? I mean, that orgasm thing, that is one powerful experience, wouldn't you say? Well, it had to be. Sex has always been in competition with hunger. And by hunger I don't mean a little peckishness around tea time, brother. I mean agonizing, constant, miserable hunger. I mean crippling emptiness that turns people and animals into vicious destroyers. Famine, Dan. Famine is the theme song of the world. In famine people will eat anything.

DAN: Anything? You're implying—

FERGUS: Hunger is a dreadful, dreadful, dreadful way to die. To avoid that—

DAN: Cannibalism is what you mean. But if—

FERGUS: Everyone alive today is the great-grandchild of a cannibal. Of someone who decided to eat and live. You may have to go back five hundred thousand years or more—to the first hominid with intelligence. But somewhere along the line there was an ancestor who ate the flesh of his tribe. And knew it was the flesh of his tribe. Of course, you need only go back to 1944, say, and the siege of Leningrad. Thousands were eaten there. We have always been enslaved by hunger. It's hard to accept now, in New York, in this modern time, where hamburgers grow on trees. But cannibalism is what sex is all about.

DAN: What do you mean? Sex is all about?

FERGUS; Sex is a *cover*. The story we tell about sex—all our complexes and desires and myths—that isn't the deep dark side of us. Not at all. Compared to the mysteries of eating—compared to the terrible, scary mysteries of cannibalism—sex is a pretty modern invention. A magic ritual, rather. A ceremony. A distraction from the great guilt.

DAN: That we ate another human being.

FERGUS: Sex conserves. Sex, in fact, encourages temperance in eating. Sex says, "Don't kill and eat this person. If you kill her there will be none left for tomorrow. Substitute this great, pleasurable act—screwing—for your terrible desire to kill and eat. At least for now, spare her. Tomorrow your hunger may be too great. But for now spare her."

DAN: So what you are saying is that—

FERGUS: It's the male orgasm that saves the female's life. Over and over again. Sex is always battling with hunger. Battling against the kill-eat drive. Sex is trying to keep the species alive. Offering pleasure and affection instead of that deadly, raging, *daily* hunger. And offering a story that can hide the creature's sad and shameful memory of its cannibal acts. God, I need a Coke. My spit's like glue.

DAN: Waiter. With ice?

FERGUS: Yuh.

DAN: Coke with ice.

WAITER: Coke with ice. Your fifth burger is coming.

FERGUS: Make up a half dozen burgers to go.

DAN: Why? I've got plenty of food at home.

FERGUS: I can't go with you. I'm not, you know—

WAITER: I'll be back.

DAN: Not what?

FERGUS: I'm not fit to live with just now.

DAN: Well, so we'll clean you up. I said that.

FERGUS: I mean I'm not house-trained. I'm feral.

DAN: Nonsense.

FERGUS: Okay, I mean... I'm not always... well, there are times when I tune out. When I go into some kind of psycho spasm. I don't remember where I am. I scare people on the streets. I'm insane a lot, is what I'm saying.

DAN: Lousy diet probably.

FERGUS: This cannibalism *shtick*—it's obsessing me. I'm finding all these, you know, *correspondences* between sex and eating. Every aspect of our sexuality matches up with some aspect of eating. Covers it. I feel very lonely thinking this way. Doesn't it all sound crazy to you?

DAN: No more than usual. Remember the first night we met, that time on the freezing D train? You told me the Garden of Eden was in the female's reproductive tract.

FERGUS: But that—that's kind of optimistic. This, the eating thing, it makes me sad.

DAN: Are you talking about Neanderthals and Cro-Magnon's and like that? The beginnings of man?

FERGUS: That's the problem, you've put your finger on the problem. That's the reason we humans get so screwed up. "In the beginning—" But there is no beginning, no single start for man. There are many beginnings and all of them important. All of them piled one atop the other in the Collective Unconscious. None of them really forgotten. All competing for our attention. There's the mythic beginning—called Genesis in the Judeo-Christian world. There's the physical beginning—mother's egg bouncing down to be fertilized. And the psychological beginning when an infant first starts imposing coherence on the strange new world of sight and sound. But that's not all. There's the beginning when our first hominid ancestor evolved into us. And another beginning when that Dawn Species first knew intelligence. We're wrapped in this ball of our beginnings. We don't know where to start. People start at different places—that's how come we don't understand each other.

DAN: And which beginning is the cannibal beginning?

FERGUS: They all are.

DAN: Oh, dear.

FERGUS: That's right, it could get you down. Even in our biological beginning, in such a primitive moment as that—one male sperm will kill another male sperm while swimming to the egg. Maybe these are instances of cannibal sperm, I wouldn't be surprised. Biologists refer to cannibal cells.

WAITER: Number five. Did you decide about the take-out order?

DAN: Uh.

FERGUS: Indulge me. I feel insecure unless I squirrel something away.

DAN: Make six burgers to go. And more coffee.

FERGUS: Thanks.

DAN: After this, after the coffee, we'll get a cab and go out to Brooklyn. Promise me that.

FERGUS: I can't.

DAN: Why not? You have a job interview or something?

FERGUS: Because it won't be good for us. Right now—aside from this meal I owe you, we're on even terms.

DAN: If we don't get along, if I can't hack your living with me, then I'll throw you out, I promise. Stop the pride thing.

FERGUS: I have no pride.

DAN: Yes, you do. You're especially proud about how humble you've become. You want to be the quintessential homeless man. You revel in it. The dirt, the smell, the misery.

FERGUS: Anything worth doing is worth doing well.

DAN: You love it. You're the most arrogant bum I've every met. It's standing in the way of your salvation.

FERGUS: Okay, stop. That's enough.

DAN: Well—

FERGUS: I have these fits. What they call episodes. I'm not always sure who I am. Not even certain what state of being I'm in. I seem to... I can go from... How to put this? I have an incredible ability—or is it a need? Or is it both? I have an incredible ability to empathize, to meld into another state of human existence. And when this happens—it's very scary—I'm not sure I'm Fergus anymore. All right, it's scary but it's also exciting. It's almost an ecstatic moment. And I require it. It makes me feel connected. I don't want to be around someone who thinks I'm crazy just now. I can't afford that. I've got to believe in my visions.

DAN: You've told me about trances before. About how you discovered the Theophysical Universe—and I don't think you're crazy.

FERGUS: But this is different, this is primal. This hurts.

DAN: In what way?

FERGUS: It deals with all levels of human consciousness, it is the one theme that holds true for very aspect of our evolution.

DAN: What does?

FERGUS: Cannibalism.

DAN: Oh.

FERGUS: See? You'd rather not hear this.

DAN: No, no. Go on.

FERGUS: All right. Start with the first beginning, the beginning of beginnings, start with the primal soup. That moment when six atoms or sixteen atoms came together—and, all of a sudden, some vague electricity began to connect atom with atom with atom. A vague electricity called life. And with it came a vague fear. That the atoms of the First Organism would come apart and the electricity would no longer be connected. That the First Organism would disintegrate and die. The perception of life brings with it the perception of death.

DAN: I've no problem with that.

FERGUS: Now the First Organism didn't have anything like intelligence—it just wanted to continue. Six or sixteen things—carbon things and oxygen things and hydrogen things—six or sixteen things together are better than those six or sixteen things apart. Electricity flows and gives sensual delight. It flows, but the First Organism didn't know why. As a result everything in the primal soup threatened it. Movement threatened it. The approach of other things and other substances threatened it. The First Organism was paranoid. Why not? This was a new experience. What the First Organism most wanted was, well, for everything else "to be made still."

DAN: "To be made still" means killing?

FERGUS: That's maybe too sophisticated. There's hardly any life so there's hardly any death. Most of what the First Organism drove away or absorbed was dead matter anyway. But, in time, other organisms with electricity did appear. And competed. And had "to be made still." And in the process these first organisms learned a kind of pleasure. When things were still—if only for a moment—there was peace. Not only that: useful parts of the enemy were absorbed. And incorporated. The six or sixteen piece thing developed into a sixty piece thing. A primitive form of eating began. And a primitive form of famine and scarcity began. If two organisms had absorbed, say, all the available free radicals in an area, then one organism would have to cannibalize another. The kill-eat mechanism was established.

DAN: And where does sex come in?

FERGUS: Sex, as I've said, counteracts the kill-eat urge. Sex and reproductivity are caused by attraction. When the electricity of one thing and the electricity of another thing are drawn together—positive to negative—then those things can unite to form a double thing. Maybe the positive charge is primordial maleness and the negative charge is primordial femaleness. Or vice versa. But, whatever the moment was—when the positive and the negative cancelled each other out— that moment of completion is what we call orgasm today.

DAN: I suppose.

FERGUS: There was always a dreadful tension between the kill-eat instinct and the more sophisticated urge to have orgasm and reproduce. And that tension has followed man through every stage of evolution. Through every beginning. Even though, for most of the time (and especially now), we've been in a major state of denial about it.

WAITER: Six burgers to go. Will there be anything else?

DAN: Fergus?

FERGUS: Whatever it takes to finish what I'm saying. Some apple pie.

WAITER: Apple pie. I'll bring your check.

DAN: I'm not rushing you—

FERGUS: It's just a little bit more. The Dawn People. I want to tell you about the Dawn People.

DAN: Prehistoric man.

FERGUS: Yes and no. The cave people you're probably thinking of—they came later. Even Lucy came later. They already had a rudimentary intelligence. The Dawn People, they belong in the moment when intelligence was just beginning. On and off. Maybe it took 50,000 years, that moment. On and off. It's like what they call the hypnagogic state, between sleeping and waking, between consciousness and no-consciousness. It was what you'd call the hypnagogic state of the human species—where visions come. Scary visions. When Dawn Man first knew that he was separate from the group, an individual. There was "me" and "you" and "they." Bones of the Dawn People have not been discovered. Will never be.

DAN: So how can you describe them then?

FERGUS: They were hungry and they were just beginning to be intelligent, off and on. There must have been such people. One day we began to be conscious. And *all* days we have been hungry. So there must have been a time when hungry, just-conscious Dawn People existed. Had to be.

DAN: Okay. I grant that for the sake of argument.

FERGUS: Let me take you back to a hot day on the savannah, however many million years ago. Pay attention now—I've worked it all out very painstakingly. A hot day. And there's this thick-headed Dawn Man, let's call him Dan. Dan's walking along and he spots a Dawn Female, a female he's never seen before. Call her Bea. Dan sees Bea, she doesn't see him, and Dan ducks behind a bush. What's he gonna do?

DAN: You tell me.

FERGUS: Well, first of all, Dan tries to think. This isn't so easy since Dan is only intelligent half the time. The other half is made up of instinct and smell and chemical response and whatever happens to your cat when it gets scared and its tail blows up like a feather boa. Because primitive Dan, like your cat, is scared. Try to imagine it. A hot day.

DAN: Go on.

FERGUS: So. Dan is wondering—if he can do such a complex thing as wonder—Dan feels, Dan senses, Dan thinks, "Is this other Dawn Person a danger to me?" Without being clear about it, he thinks, "Does this other Dawn Person have kinsmen hiding around here who will kill me?" "Is this other Dawn Person going to eat all the fruit and starve me out? "Is this other Dawn Person going to pick up a rock and crush my skull with it while I'm sleeping?" And, as fear shuffles around in Dan's mind, Bea starts to do something that is really intolerable.

DAN: She goes shopping.

FERGUS: No, smart-ass, Bea is *moving*. Dan has gotten all paranoid, just like the First Organism did, because he feels threatened by her movement. Somehow he has "to make her still." So Dan comes out from behind his bush. He runs forward and attacks the other Dawn Person.

DAN: Go on.

FERGUS: At that moment Dan's psychological need—I must "make her still"— gets mixed up with his physiological need. The need to have sex and reproduce. As Dan starts to strangle Bea, he also starts to have an erection. Her warmth, her wonderful raunchy smell. The friction of body on body. Instinctively his cock enters her vagina. The only question is this—the question that always lies just under the surface of human screwing. No matter how convincingly we deny it.

DAN: You have my attention. What's the question?

FERGUS: The question is this: which will win the race? The orgasm or death? Will Dan strangle Bea? Or will his orgasm come first? Because, because— what did I tell you before?

DAN: Oh. It's the male orgasm that saves the female's life.

FERGUS: No man entering a woman—then or now—knows for sure whether he's screwing her or killing her.

DAN: Isn't that a bit extreme?

FERGUS: Sex is extreme. My God what a weird, violent, thrusting business it is. The male shoves his hard drumstick into the intestines of the female. Or so it seems. Into her most vulnerable part. Repeatedly. While the woman is screaming. How can you distinguish that from death? And, what's worse, she often bleeds.

DAN: Bea yells, "Kill me, kill me." My Bea, that is.

FERGUS: *Quod erat demonstrandum.* And, from this, what can we assume about female evolution?

DAN: Ah. Ah—the sexiest woman survived.

FERGUS: Yes. Exactly. Very good. If the male orgasm saves the female's life, then—well, the woman who fetches out orgasms best will not be killed. The female who lubricates most efficiently will have a better chance of getting Dan's rocks off in time to save her life. And what else? What does an orgasm resemble, as we've just been saying?

DAN: Death.

FERGUS: Death. Because primitive Dan, that nincompoop, doesn't know what happened. He doesn't know what death is. That's too intellectual a concept for him. Dan only wants "to make her still." And that's what God created the orgasm to simulate. Violent motion. A lot of screaming and fingernails down the spine. Then stillness. Dawn women, if they had to, faked their orgasms. It was probably the first imaginative act.

DAN: The first fantasy role-playing. The first psychodrama.

FERGUS: In any case, the woman is "made still." She is no longer threatening. Dan can abide her presence, if she doesn't move. And if the orgasm came first, if she is alive—then, in time, Dan will say, "You got a cigarette?"—

DAN: And, if it doesn't work out, if the orgasm doesn't come in time? If she dies? What does he do? Does he eat her?

FERGUS: Sometimes. Sometimes yes and sometimes no. Depends on how hungry he is. If it's famine time, old Dan doesn't really have a choice. He may feel uneasy about it, when he's in an intelligent mode. But when he's not smart, well, then his nose will dictate what he does. His nose says, "This flesh is good to eat." Then his nose sets off some hunger pangs in his stomach and it's all over. One thing any expert on the subject of cannibalism will agree about—

DAN: Rhetorical question.

FERGUS: Human flesh tastes good.

DAN: Like chicken.

FERGUS: Like pork. So there is no natural aversion to cannibalism. Nature didn't make one human unappetizing to another human. Nature could have, I suppose. But it didn't. Maybe nature decided that cannibalism—occasional cannibalism at least—is useful for the species.

DAN: How could cannibalism increase Dawn Man's chances? Wouldn't it decrease evolutionary success—by introducing another source of danger?

FERGUS: There's lots of ways to figure it. Cannibalism may increase the socialization of a species—for the sake of self-defense. The first protection rackets begin. You don't eat me, I don't eat you. In certain animal species cannibalism helps to disperse the adolescent members of the tribe in an orderly manner over time. "We better take a powder, Uncle Ugh is looking at us in that hungry way again." And then, of course, cannibalism supplies extra food. Remember cannibalism doesn't necessarily mean murder. People die. Their bodies are eaten. It makes economic sense. Maybe we succeeded in the Darwinian way *because* we were cannibals. Because we weren't too fastidious when it came to eating our own in the famine time.

DAN: You picture the female as victim. What's going on in Bea's head?

FERGUS: Well, before I get into the female mind-set, let me make a stipulation. We have to remember, when I say male or female, we have to remember that there is male and female *in each of us.* The aggressive and the submissive, in each of us. Especially as intelligence gets more and more sophisticated.

DAN: But do you say that the female needs to be killed and to be eaten?

FERGUS: This is touchy. I have to be careful here. "Needs" is maybe the wrong word. The female has, oh, a kind of fatalism about it. She's smaller, weaker. It's more likely that she will be killed—that her body will in time supply nutrients for the entire group. The fetus will live off her—cannibalizing her body for calcium and vitamins—even if the tribe doesn't actually eat her. Women feed us. But, to avoid a violent, wasteful death, women have invented this magic ritual, this play-acting. This dance of life. I will allow you to stab me with your penis. I will scream and die. You will be satisfied. You will not fear me. And after a while I will awake to life again. But now there will be a little sea of sperm inside me.

DAN: Come live with me and be my love. And we will all the pleasures prove.

FERGUS: Because the male has learned how "to make the female still." And without killing her. Unless he's very, very hungry. Famine hungry. Starved, malnourished man, as I told you, can't get an erection anyway. There is no penis, no magic wand to save the female's life. If times are *really* bad, the female will even be eaten alive.

DAN: Uhhh.

FERGUS: It happened. Don't think about it. I guess I'll have a burger. Talked myself into another appetite.

> [*Just then the waiter returned with my change. I laid a huge tip on him. Fergus was preoccupied: he had begun to eat a hamburger from his doggie bag. He was humming, the sort of human purr that comes with gastrointestinal satisfaction. The waiter said, "Thank you." Then, leaning down as he pushed crumbs around, he whispered, "My brother's a schizophrenic, too."*

> *And I thought, "Can that be all?" Is all this nothing more than the peep and mutter of a routine madness? Fergus's "visions," could they just be a call for lithium? Well, of course, Fergus was insane. But I reserved to myself (however crazily) a reader's judgment. Sane or insane, if something had a compelling structure and an organic presence—if it obeyed a logic of its own— then, as metaphor at least, it deserved attention. I was very unsure of my faith, you understand. And defensive about my intellectual unrootedness. When Bea quoted the New Testament, I quoted Fergus. And so, naturally, I again asked him to come home and live with me.*

> *I was that ticked off at Bea.*

> *Fergus didn't say yes. But, for the first time, he didn't say no either. He temporized. (My first tape had run out, so I don't recall the exact tone of his voice.) Fergus, it seems, had stashed a sheaf of manuscript notes somewhere in town. He couldn't leave for Brooklyn without his notes. I said—no problem— that I would accompany him to the hiding place. Fergus said he couldn't think of inconveniencing me—the place didn't open until six. (It was not four then.) And, moreover, if I came with him, we'd have to buy new D batteries for Fergus's flashlight. That remark, I must say, did not encourage me.*

> *In retrospect, I think, Fergus had already decided to give me the slip—he wasn't interested in letting an X-generation drop-out do some kind of Good Samaritan act on his behalf. But he hadn't finished talking. That was his great*

weakness: it transcended sex and cannibalism. It was, as far as I could tell, the exception that proved all his rules. Fergus had to talk. Talk was his only decent suit of clothes.

So he maneuvered me into following him up Washington Street and east over to Greenwich (after I had bought batteries, many Snickers bars, a six-pack of Coke and more tape for me). It was a short walk—Fergus wouldn't let me call a cab—but his right foot began to drag after just one block. A Kleenex thickness of snow had fallen while we were at Peronista's. His left foot made a sharp outline. His right foot was just an undifferentiated scuff. I suggested the emergency room at St. Vincent's. But he said, "No, no." It would be easier to get things looked at in Brooklyn. I should have known then that Fergus was blowing me off.

He led me to, of all places, a Catholic church: St. Nerva's, built in 1887 as an outreach to teamsters and longshoremen. I hadn't noticed it there before. The facade, its rose window maybe excepted, would have been appropriate to a warehouse. Under each overhang and sill in the factory-red brick wall there were chalky stalactites of efflorescence. The front entrance, which was open, looked like a loading dock, as if Christianity were a product to be stored or processed there. Fergus slid his JETS hat off, then he turned to me and put one finger across his upper lip. The church was almost sensuous inside. Late western light played down through an ovate clear glass dome in which the dove of the Holy Spirit, the one colorful image, flew. This clear light gave the shapely marble columns a veining and a certain naked musculature: each column seemed to "make a leg" as Renaissance courtiers might. Around the walls, paintings and statuary projected a menstrual redness against the chocolaty wood. Jesus on the cross seemed something of an exhibitionist. He tried to catch my eye. It was a very European place.

Silence, it turned out, was not required. A cleaning woman, St. Nerva's third occupant, vacuumed at the high altar. Her back was to us. She didn't see Fergus pull me along the far side aisle. There were four confessionals, like

148

bathing stalls, along the wall. When we reached the last one Fergus brusquely shoved me through a curtain, into the penitent's seat. He then entered on the confessor's side. A panel slid open and I could see his profile through the grillwork.

"What's this prank about?" I asked. And I flipped my tape recorder on.]

FERGUS: We can hang out here for a while.

DAN: In the confessional? Why can't we go sit in a pew?

FERGUS: They prefer it if I don't —like, you know—I'm not too desirable in my present condition. And I don't feel at ease talking out there.

DAN: They? Who's they?

FERGUS: Mostly an old drinking buddy named Roger. He's the sexton. He lets me come and go from the basement here, if I don't make a big production out of it. So I try to pick my spots.

DAN: But suppose someone comes in? Someone who really wants to confess?

FERGUS: The priests don't get here 'til seven usually. Roger will go on duty at least an hour before that. Ha, actually, now that you mention it, that did happen to me once. Someone sat where you're sitting. I was asleep on this side.

DAN: What did he say? I mean when you told him you weren't a priest?

FERGUS: Well, he'd already started confessing. He was very upset. And a bit hyper—I was afraid he'd get mad, yank me out of here, and clean my clock. So I just went with the flow. Tried to give him good advice.

DAN: What was he confessing to?

FERGUS: He'd eaten an eight pound chocolate cake.

DAN: Eaten a cake? That's all?

FERGUS: It was supposed to be his daughter's birthday cake. He ate it the night before. He was miserable with shame. A compulsive over-eater, I think. He couldn't control himself. It was a serious matter, don't underestimate it.

DAN: What did you say?

FERGUS: What could I say? I forgave him. And I told him that eating his daughter's birthday cake was better than eating his daughter. I don't think he understood me. Maybe it's just as well he didn't.

DAN: He was—you think—he was acting out some sexual fantasy?

FERGUS: Sex covers eating. And, in return, eating covers sex. Back and forth we go. When they can't cope with sex, men and women make up stories about food. When they can't cope with food, men and women make up stories about sex. Back and forth, back and forth.

DAN: Maybe I preferred the old Oedipus story. Wanting to kill your father and sleep with your mother.

FERGUS: Oh, it's about that, too. Sure. But that's not all it's about. Sex is a real thing, a dark thing—that doesn't mean it's the first thing or the most important thing. First comes eating. Even Freud—Mr. Sex—had a vague idea of this. Remember how it goes? The primordial Father, according to Freud, drives his adolescent male children out of the tribe so that Dad can have the women to himself. The kids rise up and kill him. But that's not all they do. They also eat him, Freud says. For many reasons, hunger being not the least. Out of fear, out of anger. To absorb his power. Whatever. But Freud didn't go far enough.

DAN: Hold on. Let me get his straight. I'm a little confused. Who is Oedipus in all this?

FERGUS: He's the archetypal adolescent son or sons. Driven out of the tribe. Freud separates the two stories—the Oedipus story and the story of the archetypal adolescent kids—but they're really the same story. One's on the level of the psyche, of art, dressed up so that we can face the horror of it. You know: Laius,

150

Oedipus's father, hears from an oracle that Oedipus will kill him. So he abandons the infant Oedipus to die. (That is, he drives Oedipus out of the tribe.) Oedipus grows up, meets his father, but doesn't recognize him, and kills him in a fair fight. The other story occurs on a pre-historical, tribal, visceral level. It's a much nastier business. On the tribal level the father is killed *and* he is eaten. Even the ancient Greeks had blocked that memory. The story of Oedipus, as told by Sophocles, is civilized and modern, pretty much. Sophocles's Oedipus is too sophisticated to eat his father. The Oedipus story, dressed up as a parable of our sexual relationship with Mom and Dad, well, it camouflages, it covers the primal truth about a cannibalistic act that must have occurred millions and millions of times in hominid history. A commonplace thing. The tribe must move along. The old die, even when they're not murdered. The tribe must use available protein efficiently. Waste not, want not. And if there's famine in the land—well, then anything goes.

DAN: And we repress that fact? The eating part.

FERGUS: Um, that's not all we repress. Eating Laius isn't all we repress. That, in fact, is the easy part. It's much darker than that. Much more horrifying than that. Want a Snickers bar?

DAN: Not just now.

FERGUS: Mmmm.

DAN: You're playing this for the effect.

FERGUS: Actually, I'm scared to tell you. I'm afraid you'll think I'm paranoid schizophrenic. But it makes sense. If you accept the fact that hunger has been the driving force—the amoral, unrelenting force—since Day One onward. If you accept that—well…

DAN: What do I have to accept?

FERGUS: That we all remember, in the Collective Unconscious—we all remember eating Mother, too. Not just Dad.

DAN: I can't go that far.

FERGUS: Who can? It's the most appalling secret of the human heart. The person we love most, depend on most. It's an intolerable thought. Absolutely intolerable. But, don't forget. Sex covers eating. Oedipus has intercourse with Jocasta—he even has children by her.

DAN: But really he doesn't have sex? Really he kills Jocasta and eats her?

FERGUS: Yes and no. We are all of these things. At the same time. And at different times. Our Unconscious is so layered, so profoundly fouled up, that it's a wonder we can function at all. It's a great tribute to the human spirit. Those adolescent males, they took over the tribe and fertilized their own mothers. That must have happened again and again. Survival of the tribe required it. It could not be otherwise. But there was also the terrible need for protein. Mother, like father, must die some day of old age—then mother, like father, will become part of the available food supply. And she will be eaten.

DAN: *Killed* and eaten?

FERGUS: Sometimes. Probably not killed as often as the father is killed. Mother doesn't threaten us as much as father does. But at times—yes—mother was put out of her misery if she became old and useless. And was eaten. Mind now, she might even have welcomed it. Mothers' sacrifice themselves. If famine threatens the young and the productive members of the tribe—then she might offer herself. Out of love.

DAN: Talk about guilt trips.

FERGUS: And with it comes an even more frightening collective thought. That we are all just the sum—no more, no less—of our available calories. Under the right circumstances (or the wrong circumstances, like famine), we're all reduced to food. It is our worth. There are plenty of modern examples—the Donner party, the Andes plane crash, the Bay of Pigs boat people. But, in general, we avoid thinking about such matters. We stop at the level of sex, because to call up the

152

kill-eat world, to remember it, is to engage madness. Education, civility, love, all those things go out the window when there is no food.

DAN: Actually that's not so hard to take. Being eaten. As long as it doesn't hurt. I just can't deal with the idea of eating my mother.

FERGUS: But, Dan. Dan, you started eating your mother the day you were conceived.

DAN: You mean by that—?

FERGUS: Think about it. I gotta nosh a bit. Didn't we get any Cokes?

[Fergus—I hear it on the tape—started to rattle his paper bag. The smell of burgers fused with the smell of him: I almost barfed all over the confessional. The whole set-up was ridiculous—priest and sinner. But it had an effect on me. The darkness provided a modest kind of sensory deprivation. Fergus's voice, disembodied, had authority (separated, as it was, from his rag coat and yellow eyes). His intellectual attack had been absolutely relentless. I could imagine Fergus staggering as he walked block after block, night after night, in the snow, rehearsing his convoluted argument. He'd gotten it down pat. Twice before, after all, I had seen Fergus in this obsessive, free-associative mode of expression. By now I knew enough not to contradict him.

And, yes, I was titillated by it all. Resistant, angry, frightened, worn down, fascinated, too. Fergus's standing on the planet was, God knows, precarious, and that gave him clout, or so it seemed to me when I thought about it later. Desperate men are allowed to have desperate insights. A last meal, you might say. But more: Fergus, I sensed, was making me a bequest of his ideas. What he told me that afternoon was in anticipation of death. And it gave both of us a peculiar license. For him to speak about horror. For me to hear it.

But you have made no such commitment. You can put this book down now. And maybe you should do so. For what follows is even more terrible—more gruesome and sad—than what has gone before.]

FERGUS: So where were we?

DAN: I'd rather not think about that. It makes me an accomplice.

FERGUS: Eating mother. Yes.

DAN: Can't we skip that part? When's your friend coming? It's five-twenty. Aren't they gonna think it's strange, this long-winded confession?

FERGUS: We're alone, the cleaning lady left at five. We're locked in. You can pull the curtain back if you want. Dan—

DAN: Have you got this all written down somewhere? It'd be easier—I could control it more—if I read it off a piece of paper in, say, Brooklyn. Someplace. Please?

FERGUS: Listen to you. Like everyone else, you don't want to hear it. The truth. Look, I can't blame you, it's hard. Very hard. But, believe me, there is no Christian redemption without this truth. There is no understanding without this truth. This is what the primal sin must have been. If you don't know what your sin is, then you can never repent, and you can never be forgiven.

DAN: Eating Mother, that's the primal sin?

FERGUS: In our minds at least, it is. I mean, what more terrible thought could there be? Huh? That we are alive because others have died. Died and their bodies scavenged for nourishment. Not just bodies. Bodies of the people we love most. And we savored them. Saliva of appetite formed in our mouths. We had second helpings. And we hate ourselves for it. We've blocked all reference to that memory. It's too awful to contemplate. That's what I'm trying to make you do—

DAN: Contemplate it?

FERGUS: Yes. Because—because. If you see it clearly, you will also see the extenuating circumstances clearly. And if you see them clearly, then maybe you can forgive yourself. Or, if not forgive, then you can have compassion for yourself—for the primitive animal who wept while it gnawed the flesh of its mother.

DAN: Fergus. How do you propose to do this?

FERGUS: Well. It's simple. What I'm going to do is take the whole story of our sexuality—and lift up its skirts, so to speak. Positions, customs, fantasies, fetishes. Neuroses and superstitions, the whole sexual megillah. If I can show you how every aspect of our sexuality is a cover for eating, item by item by item, if I can do that, then perhaps you'll be brave enough to look behind the mystery. To the more important mystery.

DAN: Go ahead. I know I'll regret it, but go ahead.

FERGUS: Great. You're a sport. So. So. Where's the best place to start? Yes, at the breast, at mother's breast. That's the most enigmatic and mysterious part of the female anatomy.

DAN: Isn't the—uh, the other part... Isn't that more mysterious? It's more mysterious to me.

FERGUS: I know what you mean. But the breast we tend to take for granted. And we shouldn't. It feeds us. Not just the male child, but the female child as well. Its power over mankind is universal. The breast is sacred. A magic place. We eat it, yet it's never consumed. Nursing is the first cannibal act.

DAN: But it isn't really. A cannibal act.

FERGUS: So you say. Now. At age 35. With all your adult reasoning. But little Dan, the infant, little Dan, the child—what does he know about it? He only knows that mother's flesh will feed him somehow. That's all. Mostly the nipple. He sucks and chews, chews hard, and nourishment comes out. How? Why? Later on he will chew meat and devour it with the same jaw motions. The meat is eventually eaten and it vanishes. But the breast is never eaten. It's the great fertile cornucopia. It's also the place of safety and of love.

DAN: I was weaned early, somehow I was allergic to my mother's milk. So for years I'd suck my thumb and, you know, rub my forefinger around the tip of my nose. God, that felt good. Made great alpha waves in my brain or something.

The thumb was my mother's nipple, of course, and the forefinger was the rest of her tit brushing gently against my nose as her breath rose and fell.

FERGUS: You're probably right.

DAN: I'd do it now, if I had the guts. Sit on the D train and suck my thumb. Cheaper than chewing gum. Women get off on it, get off on breast feeding, from what I'm told.

FERGUS: Sure. That's nature saying, "Hmmm. This won't work. How can I possibly convince the female to put up with three years' worth of painful chest-biting—never mind she has to carry the little brat around? Aha. Got it. I'll give her dynamite orgasms while she's nursing. It'll be our little secret." Ta-da, the durable and patient nursing mother was created.

DAN: Durable and horny.

FERGUS: Naturally, for the child, all this presents some exciting and confusing information. Probably, at that point, the infant has more power over his or her mother's sexual response system than father has. And both male infants and female infants give pleasure to mom how? By doing what?

DAN: Phrase that again?

FERGUS: Okay. I guess I should put it this way. What does the infant *think*— from its perspective? With its limited data-bank? Well, it thinks, "Hmmm. Looks like Mom is getting her rocks off. Gosh, how am I giving her this pleasure? How?"

DAN: By eating her.

FERGUS: Give the man a cigar. Mother—the infant thinks—is turned on when I eat her. That's good. But, in time, a troubling ambivalence sets in. The infant feels guilt. Pleasurable as it might have been, the infant knows—as it becomes a social animal— *That it wanted to devour its mother.* It didn't do so. Something intervened. Somehow the nipple wasn't eaten. A miracle. But no thanks to the infant. The infant knows hunger already. The infant knows also that—if it could have, if—it would have wolfed the mother down whole. Yet, yet—it loves mom. And so this black conundrum festers in the brain—"How could I have loved my mother and wanted—yearned—to eat her at the same time?" This is horror as Kurtz sees horror in *Heart of Darkness*. It infuses all of us. We begin our lives in contemplation of cannibalism. And if I can eat my own mother, well, then, can't I be eaten, too? *Shouldn't* I be eaten, too? Don't I deserve to be eaten? I ate her vital fluids in the womb. I chewed her as an infant. What's to keep her from eating *me* up?

DAN: Sex covers eating, as you say. The mother's orgasm covers the pain of the little cannibal chewing her nipple.

FERGUS: Exactly. And well put. The first pang of hunger in the child leads to a sexual response in the mother. From the beginning. But we're not finished with the female breast.

DAN: No?

FERGUS: Some day, remind me to tell you why men have nipples. I can't go into it now. But the breast. What else is the female breast?

DAN: Don't test me, I'm tired. What *else* is it?

FERGUS: A deposit of edible fatty tissue.

DAN: Ugh. Edible? No way.

FERGUS: Dan, you react like that because you live in a society where animal fat is available. Probably too available. I don't think Dawn Men and Dawn Women had high cholesterol. Fat is essential. Without fat you can't store nourishment. You die. It was hard to hunt and kill a fat-bearing animal. Maybe weeks would go by. The sight of a female breast would begin to excite hunger. Why d'you think so many men are proud to have big-busted girlfriends? Because large breasts represent a rich store of fat. Represent wealth.

DAN: But you don't eat your wife's breasts, for God sake.

FERGUS: You try not to. Certainly you try not to. Instead you eat that more common form of cannibal feast. Captives. Those men and women from weaker tribes, those defeated in battle. It's my assumption here that in times of famine— or to prepare for times of famine—the strong kept the weak as we keep cattle. Food on the hoof. It allowed the tribe to have a certain flexibility. If food was plentiful, then the captive survived. In time, he or she might be integrated into the tribe. But, if scarcity struck—at least there was a convenient, mobile supply of nourishment. And, when fat was hard to get, the captive's breast was particularly attractive.

DAN: Good God, what a bleak picture.

FERGUS: It was a bleak time. For hundreds of thousands of years. Try to picture it, feel it. Use your imagination. Imagine waking up on a cold, grassy plain—with your naked, malnourished tribe sprawled around you. There's been nothing to eat for days. You're too weak to hunt. You whimper from the merciless, gnawing pain of hunger. Your mouth is scabbed. And then one of your tribe, a female, staggers to her feet. And the first sunlight shines on her breasts. They're beautiful. And they remind you of food. It's simple logic. I'm not trying to sensationalize it. You're *dying* of hunger, remember that.

DAN: I suppose it makes some ruthless sense. Stupid, ruthless sense. Sickening.

FERGUS: The female breast fascinates the male. But, primarily, if you think about it, as a visual object. That's why men don't mind when women get a silicone job—even though siliconed breasts are about as sexy to the touch as rocks. Men respond to the sight of breasts. What they look like. Big breasts are a sign of fruitfulness, of nursing-potential, of fat content. But, in the sex act itself, the breast is really a secondary trait. More a center of erotic pleasure for the female than for the male. As a sexual organ the breast is strangely muted. We try to incorporate the breast into the sex act because we want sex to cover the truth— that the breast was once considered to be a potential source of food. And I don't mean just milk.

DAN: To kill the female by eating her breast—isn't that un-economical?

FERGUS: Who says it killed her necessarily? Woman live after mastectomies.

DAN: I'm sick.

FERGUS: Of course, you'd be less likely to remove the breast of a nursing mother—one that could provide you with milk even after, say, her child was killed. And that would be an incentive for captive woman—for her to breed. She's more valuable to the tribe as a cow, so to speak.

DAN: Where's love? That's what I want to know.

FERGUS: Love is for a time of plenty. Famine requires brutal measures. Of course what I've told you is sickening. That's why it's buried so deeply in our brains, under the comparatively gentle disguise of sex. Men today act out the hungry male hominid's ancient response. He sees the breast. If the hominid is attracted to its potential as food, then he fondles the breast to gauge its weight and tone. Then he sucks on it to see if this woman is a nursing mother. If not, then...

DAN: Then—

FERGUS: Well, once upon a time, he might have eaten the breast. Today, though, the sex act has supplanted the cannibal act. The breast has become part of the foreplay. Modern man then quickly moves on to the genital area, on to the act of intercourse. Again the male orgasm has saved the female's breast. By distracting the cannibal urge.

DAN: God help us all.

FERGUS: So, in the darkest time, in the years of woe, some male or some female had to eat the mother's breast. There was no other option, no time for love or squeamishness. Mother, say, had died—whether a natural death or an accidental death. If the hominid didn't eat his or her mother—well, then he or she, too, would die. But think of the psychic burden. Lord, the misery and the confusion. This life force that nourished us has been devoured. So many layers of symbolism and anguish. Next time you stare reflexively at a woman's breast remember all that. It's not just rudeness, not just a sexual response. It's also an instinctive appraisal of the female as dinner. It's a hard thing to admit, but it's there.

DAN: Don't worry. I'll never look at a woman's breast again. You've ruined it for me. God, Fergus.

[*As I was saying that, the front door of St. Nerva's opened with a clunky tumbler noise. I peered out past the curtain edge. Roger, I guessed, had made his appearance—and what an appearance it turned out to be. Most of Roger was below the belt: elephantine legs, drooping abdomen and buttocks, like one of those people in the R. Crumb comic books who seem fore-shortened, giant shoes leading up to a tiny melon head. He moved (by throwing his big knees against each other) along the center aisle of the nave. Spit and gasps exploded from his mouth after each step, as if he were steam driven. His chest and arms, by comparison, seemed undeveloped. Roger had the silhouette of someone standing waist-high in a 55 gallon drum.*

Fergus popped out of the confessional to greet Roger. There followed a whining, nasal blare, elaborated with obsessive-compulsive repetitions. Roger had a Bronx accent and even fewer teeth than Fergus. To make himself understood Roger had to gather air enough so that he could blow past his flabby cheeks and lips. He wasn't always successful: so, to be on the safe side, he kept on talking through your half of the dialogue. As a result, the first part of tape 2B (I had flipped it over) is unintelligible. And I have not tried to transcribe it.

Roger—after a gummed introduction—led us back up the nave, through the vestibule, down a side staircase and into the crypt. Then along a hallway that ran, it seemed, the full length of St. Nerva's to a position just under the far apse wall. Roger unlocked a door that said MAIN ELECTRIC in faded white lettering. Fergus flipped his flashlight on. The room—lined with steam and water piping— was really the head of a long, low corridor. Roger turned and left us. I looked in. Outcrops of hard, chill Manhattan schist jutted out here and there. It seemed as if we had passed beyond the building into the native stone of the island.]

160

DAN: Go get your stuff. I'll wait here.

FERGUS: Uh. Okay. It'll take a while.

DAN: How long?

FERGUS: I'm a little slow with my leg and all. A while.

DAN: A while? How long is a while?

FERGUS: Forty minutes, maybe an hour.

DAN: What? Where are you going? To another area code?

FERGUS: Well, the path snakes around a lot. It's not direct. Just go up into the church and wait.

DAN: You'll duck out on me. I know you. Come on—I'll follow. Give me the bag, you'll need both hands.

FERGUS: You sure? You'll get your pants dirty.

DAN: It's better than talking to Roger for an hour.

FERGUS: He's really very intelligent, under all the surface noise.

DAN: I'm sure. Let's get a move on.

FERGUS: Lock the door behind you.

DAN: How do we get out again? Suppose Roger is busy upstairs?

FERGUS: There are other ways out.

DAN: Other ways?

[*But Fergus didn't answer me. He needed to ration whatever stores of breath he had. I flipped my tape machine off and followed after the bobbing light.*

It was a most peculiar trip.   We were tracing the route, Fergus told me later, of a long-disused water tunnel that—since its abandonment—had been penetrated and changed by more modern building foundations. For most of its way the tunnel was man-wide and maybe six feet in height. But there were also interruptive segments that required an awkward duck walk or the sideways tiny-step maneuver of a suicide on a building ledge. These passages often led through large rooms—one of which featured effective, witty cave paintings done in Day-Glo spray. A thin stream of water began to appear, now and then, along the route. It got quite hot: as if we were approaching some radiant source of warmth, perhaps a boiler room or a passage to the steam pipes that still heat the lower city. Sweat loosed itself all over me. Every step in and down was a step that would have to be retraced, up and out. Early on the flashlight fell and went dark. At that moment, as Fergus slowly screwed the batteries back in, I knew how dependent I was on him. And he had meant me to know: that, in part, was why he had brought me there.

We were not alone: this made me alternately optimistic and apprehensive. Some rooms served as dormitories: a certain communal order and understanding had been achieved, sanitation agreed upon. We met maybe two dozen dark figures coming along our path in the opposite direction. The narrowness of the way made for quick intimacy—I got slapped accidentally across the cheek by a whip of Rastafarian head braids. The place stank of urine and feces and an unspecific yellow smell of ancient rot. It was Fergus's particular stink, and the stink of everyone who slid past. It was becoming my signature odor. And, because of that, I eventually forgot to notice it.

Fergus was well-known: they called him "Cannibal King," which, I felt, embarrassed Fergus somewhat. The man thought a lot of himself—his outward state notwithstanding—and he didn't suffer fools gladly. He put up with me, because I coaxed and jollied him along in a flattering way—and because I had access still to the presumably "sane" world above. When you came right down to it, Fergus—like all of us—was looking for an agent.

His pad, as Fergus referred to it, was a 6 by 8 foot alcove that dead-ended in a side passage. A hot steam pipe pierced the alcove like an arrow through an apple. Some old T-shirts and a little frying pan warmed on the pipe. Fergus had

162

*three or four candle stubs, these he lit with wooden matches that lay secreted—
along with his manuscript and a bent toothbrush—behind a false cement wall.
Then he collapsed on a raggy sleeping bag. His bad leg twitched and jerked like
a full garden hose.*

*It was too hot for winter clothing. After some deliberation I took my coat
off and sat on it. After a while, when Fergus began to talk about sex and
cannibalism again, I flicked the tape recorder on.*]

FERGUS: Ah, me. Ahhh.

DAN: You make this trip every day?

FERGUS: Once a week. Ahh. At most. And usually I come in—mmph—from
an entrance that's nearer than the church. Ah. Break out the Coke. And those
Snickers bars before they turn to mush.

DAN: I think they already have. Here. How the hell you can live in a hole like
this—it's beyond my understanding. Want me to open that?

FERGUS: Okay. It has it's virtues, this place does. It's like a meditative state,
specially when there's no light. I think well down here.

DAN: There's chocolate all over your chin. To the left, more to the left. Take
the Coke. Uh-oh, your hand. What happened to the back of your hand?

FERGUS: Caught it on a piece of wire.

DAN: That's bleeding a lot.

FERGUS: It's nothing. I'll suck it clean. A little self-cannibalism. Recycle
myself. As the tribe recycled its own blood.

DAN: But your hand is filthy... What do you mean, the tribe recycled its blood?
They sucked on their wounds?

FERGUS: Mmmm. Not only did they suck on wounds to make them heal, they
even licked up menstrual blood.

DAN: What? But I thought menstruating women were unclean.

FERGUS: Oh, sure anthropologists will tell you that. But their perspective is so limited, so recent—it's hardly relevant. They're talking about modern peoples. Peoples who have already covered their unconscious memories of cannibalism with a sexual red herring or two. So, of course, to anthropologists a menstrual flow is repugnant, not clean. When, in fact, it's a useful source of protein. Especially for the children.

DAN: Oh, boy.

FERGUS: I think they were compelled to eat menstrual blood, my Dawn People were. Consider all the reasons. Blood tasted good. It was nutritious. Such substances, in a hungry time, could not be wasted. And then there was the mystical aspect of it. The vagina looks like a wound. It hemorrhages in a frightening way yet there is no death. So the Dawn People were drawn to the female genitalia both by hunger and by the desire to heal this strange wound by licking at it. Hmmm. Also it had one hell of a strong odor. You know what pheromones are?

DAN: Of course. Chemicals given off by a female that attract a male. Or vice-versa, I guess.

FERGUS: Menstruating women, it figures, gave off a powerful odor—and left an easy-to-follow spoor. Never mind the visible blood trail. That's another reason for licking up the blood. Get rid of the evidence. Don't let the women give away our position—whether the enemy is an animal or a rival hominid. Remember, smell is the most important sense. Especially at night. Hearing and sight are useless if an enemy stays silent in the dark. Only smell will give him away. Smell is the primal sense. No one—no hominid, that is—can disguise his scent. We forget that, forget what we have lost in the aroma department. Even the lowly sperm has a rudimentary sense of smell. That's how it finds the egg.

DAN: But, actually, you're making the case for a kind of uncleanness. I mean, aren't you. Smell and all?

FERGUS: I suppose. But not—or not at first—not a ritual uncleanness. Of necessity, you see, menstruating women, were kept a little separate from the tribe. That way, if the enemy followed their odor, then at least the main part of the tribe would not be surprised in an attack. So the concept of a "women's quarter" developed.

DAN: Wouldn't that make it hard for the tribe to move?

FERGUS: A little. But they could move three weeks in four. That's why women in a group, as we know, tend to synchronize their periods. For three weeks there would be little or no telltale odor. The tribe could move. Then there would be a week of rest and, with it, another nourishing discharge of blood. Men ate their mates out. As we say.

DAN: Ate their mates out. Yes—in terms of your cannibal obsession, I suppose that's a resonant way of describing it. Cunnilingus.

FERGUS: Sure. After all cunnilingus is the most obvious example of a sexual activity that covers a repressed cannibal activity. What more do you want in the way of obviousness? The vulva looks like a wound, like freshly sliced meat.

DAN: Like London broil.

FERGUS: Hmm. And once a month, yes, there actually *is* blood present just to make it look even more like a wound or a butcher's cut. Add to that the female orgasm—which evolved over time and is an exact imitation of the human death rattle. After her orgasm the woman lies inert as a fresh-killed corpse. At some deep level the woman probably knows that what she's doing is wise—acting out the role of cannibal victim. The more often she does it, the more thoroughly will the cannibal act be obscured by the sexual act. The less likely it is that the woman will actually be eaten. Instead she is "eaten out," not really eaten. Eaten symbolically. Eaten "outside" herself. Which incidentally causes orgasm.

DAN: And the guy?

FERGUS: Oh, him. Him. He—the poor sap—he doesn't know anything. He can't recognize a fake orgasm or a fake death.

DAN: Do you blame him for being confused? It's a miracle that any guy can find his crank in the dark—given the load of misleading information he wades through in a lifetime. And what about a blow-job? A blow job is a kind of eating, isn't it?

FERGUS: Sure. Today, though, we see the male as being dominant in fellatio. That wasn't always so. In the act of fellatio, a long time ago, the male hominid offered his genitals to the female as a sign of trust and mutual obligation. He endangered himself. For that one moment, at least, the woman was in power. After all, the male has put his most vulnerable parts into the female's mouth. The sexual pleasure develops *after* that—it evolves from the relief felt at having escaped mutilation.

DAN: Sperm is protein. He's giving some nourishment.

FERGUS: Yes, the male is fed on, milked. With luck he isn't castrated and cannibalized. Before even a minimal social contract could be agreed upon, the male had to know for sure that his genitals were protected. It was a constant worry. As if the Dawn Hominid didn't have enough on his mind.

DAN: Nothing changes.

FERGUS: It's remarkable. We think so highly of natural selection—how practical it is. And yet there evolves this terribly sensitive scrotum. This bag of pain. Why? Logic would say, "Make the testes as tough and defensible as walnuts. Armor them." Nature is selecting for size and strength, how come such a crucially flawed creature survived? Hell, it doesn't matter how big or strong or sharp you are. You gotta sleep. Anyone—a woman, a child—anyone could cripple or overpower even the largest male. Just grab or—better yet—bite down on the scrotum. The scrotum is the great equalizer.

DAN: So it's not a mistake? In the evolutionary process tender balls were useful?

FERGUS: Yup. Because size and strength aren't everything. Not even intelligence is enough. You got to have social skills as well. An aptitude for diplomacy. A delicate scrotum—that crucial weakness—leads to a certain statesmanship. The first article of human civility is this: "You agree not to attack my genitals, and I agree not to use my superior size and strength against you." Civilization comes from the scrotum.

DAN: I must say, the picture you paint isn't exactly romantic. Not that I'm surprised. Living here, in the damp crotch of the world—it can't be conducive to optimism. So how's about we find our way to Brooklyn now? Would that be possible? Your candles are almost out.

FERGUS: Give me a little more time. I want to stuff my shoe with newspaper.

DAN: I'm getting a mite antsy. That's all. I just saw a water bug with a saddle on it. Of course, I don't know my way, so I gotta humor you.

FERGUS: You humor me? Is that it?

DAN: No, no. I was kidding.

FERGUS: I'm some kind of eccentric at best? Some kind of monster at the worst?

DAN: No. But you have to understand. Be fair. You put people on the defensive, they don't wanna deal with killing and cannibalism. It's a natural reaction. What d'you expect? These things—if they're true, and I reserve judgment—these are hidden things. Maybe people don't want to know about them. It's like finding out you're illegitimate or something. Do you really need to know it?

FERGUS: Yes. Yes, you do.

DAN: No, Fergus. There are a lot of people—a lot—who aren't ready for this.

FERGUS: But it's a good story. A good story. It's about our miraculous transformation from predatory animal to—to a conscious being capable of love. Against all odds. Out of the void. That's a good story. I insist on it.

DAN: A good story, maybe. A cheerful story? I don't think so.

FERGUS: You're wrong, dammit. Wrong. Wrong. Wrong.

DAN: Calm down.

FERGUS: This is the heroic story. Under terrible duress, in the midst of famine and plague and drastic climate changes, still—still—human intelligence and human conscience and human charity came into being. I think it's a splendid story. And if your origins were cruel and brutal, well, then I say, all the more splendid. We've come so far. It's the human Odyssey. To discover beauty and love. Do you know what the very first definitions of beauty and love were?

DAN: No.

FERGUS: They were very simple. The definition of beauty was, "The persons or animals that are so attractive to me, smell so good to me, that I do not want to kill and eat them." And the definition of love was, "The persons or animals that I will not kill and eat because they make me feel so good emotionally." That's it. Short and sweet. But hard. For the sake of love and beauty our Dawn Ancestors risked starvation. It was a terrible choice. Terrible. To go hungry rather than to kill and eat another being. That's where God's grace and free will first join together.

DAN: Not so loud. I think someone just complained about the noise.

FERGUS: Think of the distance between snarl and smile. The physiological distance, the psychological distance. The moment when the snarl—lips pulled back, teeth bared—when the threatening snarl became the welcoming smile, that was a magical transformation. The dangerous teeth of the predator turn into the friendly, even sexual, smile of a high school cheerleader. Same facial muscles used, same dangerous teeth displayed. But now the teeth are harmless. They welcome. And kissing? Also a holdover from the cannibal dawn. Kissing developed kind of the way that handshaking would later develop— as a display of good intentions. In a handshake we say, "Look, I've got no hidden weapons." In kissing, in pressing lips and teeth together, the cannibal hominids said to each other in effect, "We are oriented face to face, I can't sneak up and bite a piece out of you from behind." Teeth were the prime weapon. In time—to cover it's origins in killing and eating— the kiss would become sexually gratifying. Erogenous zones developed around the mouth. Relief at having escaped a bite became sensual pleasure in the lips.

DAN: Also there was food to be found between the other animal's teeth.

FERGUS: Maybe that, too. Anyhow—yes, there were many crucial forks along the human evolutionary highway. None of them, none, was more decisive than the fork that led away from the primeval drive to kill and eat. And pointed instead toward a new sensibility, one that emphasized sexual reproduction and love. It was a revolution.

DAN: Was this when the hunter-gatherers settled down and started growing crops?

FERGUS: Way, way before that. In any case this new Dawn Man apparently had more reliable food sources. And with that reliable food, he had some leisure for a change. He could afford luxuries. Luxuries like a rudimentary moral sense. Maybe even an esthetic sense as well. And the first commandment was handed down inside his head, "Thou shalt not kill and cannibalize within the tribe." Of course it took thousands of years for this idea to establish itself. Every time there was a dreadful famine, well, the new man would have a relapse. Family cannibalism would occur again. But, after a long while, a long-long while, that first commandment became the defining human law. The flesh of the family was sacred. Family cannibalism was disguised as sexual incest and then rejected. Hence the Oedipus story. Screwing mom is bad. But it's a whole lot better than killing mom and then eating her. So sexual imagery came to dominate.

DAN: And cannibalism ended.

FERGUS: No, not cannibalism itself. Family cannibalism. The other kind of cannibalism went on. Still goes on.

DAN: The other kind?

FERGUS: Eating outside the family. Eating members of another tribe, say. Prisoners of war, slaves. Times were still hard. You couldn't afford to be too fastidious. You had to plan ahead. Store food up for the lean years. The best way to do that was by herding cattle. They were mobile, so the tribe could keep moving. The food stayed fresh until it was killed. If you let them, the cattle would even reproduce themselves. Ideal.

DAN: But the domestication of livestock, I think, is a pretty recent business.

FERGUS: This livestock was human.

DAN: Oh.

FERGUS: I'm down to my last burger. Talk about famine. The way I see it, our ancestors kept human flesh on the hoof. On the foot.

DAN: But there's no evidence for this. At least none I've ever heard. You're saying this was commonplace?

FERGUS: As commonplace as famine was. Very commonplace.

DAN: That's absurd. It's got to be absurd.

FERGUS: Why?

DAN: It's so—so inhuman.

FERGUS: Listen, you're talking from the McDonald's point of view. Never once in your life, probably, have you gone without food. So easy for you to judge. Such a cavalier attitude. Let them eat cake. You've got no idea what or whom you'd eat—if you went without food for a month.

DAN: Oh, now the Cannibal King is taking a high moral tone with me.

FERGUS: Well, look. Slavery existed until recently.

DAN: Plantation owners didn't eat their fieldhands.

FERGUS: No. But use your imagination. For Dawn Man slavery was a big step forward. Even being kept for food, being one individual in a human herd of cattle, was better than starving.

DAN: But then you get killed and eaten. It doesn't pay.

FERGUS: Not necessarily. There was always the hope you'd get promoted into the family—where cannibalism was forbidden and you were safe. Promoted because you got impregnated by a member of the family. Or because you had a useful skill. Meanwhile—and this is the first social contract—one man or family or tribe has taken on the task of feeding and protecting you. In return for your subordination. Suddenly men and women have value. They're at least worth their weight in calories. Doesn't sound like much, but it's the first time human beings were ranked and quantified. In slavery. Later on other qualities—strength, beauty, brains, youth—would be taken into consideration. But first, calories. On the basis of nutritive value, a slave would be taken care of, would be prized, even loved. Cattle—all kinds of cattle—were precious in the ancient world. Where do you think the desire to fondle comes from?

DAN: To fondle?

FERGUS: To touch sensually. To "feel up" as they say.

DAN: Where does it come from? It's just here, isn't it?

FERGUS: Why do you feel a woman up? Or a woman feel you?

DAN: Because. Well, I don't know how to describe it. Uh, because there are erotic zones in the fingertips. Maybe. I don't know. It's an instinctive thing. I guess. I don't know.

FERGUS: Okay, instinctive, it certainly is that. But what instinct?

DAN: Go ahead. What instinct?

FERGUS: The instinct that leads us to weigh and examine another human being for his or her potential as food. To test for fat content and muscle tone. Skin moisture. To decide where the best cuts of meat are. That's what fondling is.

And that's why we respond when fondled—we want to be found attractive. We want to be worth eating. To have high value. Subconsciously. In time, as the kill-eat instinct was being covered by the sex-love instinct, in time the body evolved sexual erotic zones that roughly correspond to the most succulent body parts. Breast, thighs, cock, buttocks and so forth. The tasty parts are the sensuous parts. The sexual nervous system—at least in the sophisticated form we know it—is a relatively late development. In the evolutionary transformation from man-as-food to man-as-sex-partner, in that transformation sensual pleasure was born. In fact, once again, it is sensual pleasure that saves us from death. That distracts us from our hunger. So buttocks are "buns." Women are "dishes" and "tomatos" and "cheesecake." Breasts are "jugs" and "sweater meat."

DAN: "I could eat you up," and all that.

FERGUS: Yes. The breast or thigh goes from being a potential meal to being a place wired for sensual pleasure. And the various time-honored sex fetishes conceal evidence of cannibalism—if you free associate a bit. Spanking and flagellation, for instance. What do they cover?

DAN: Oh.

FERGUS: Say it.

DAN: Tenderizing the meat?

FERGUS: What else? And, believe me, they needed it, tenderizing. When you think of cannibalism, you imagine eating Cindy Crawford's arm. But these were tough old birds, even the children, probably. Stringy and covered with scar tissue. Hairy. Not milk fed-veal. So you'd need to take a tree branch and swat some blood to the surface. Break up the fibers.

DAN: Is the meal alive or dead while this is happening?

FERGUS: Could be either. In fact, you might flagellate a captive regularly and never kill him. Turn him into a blood cow, break the skin and suck blood out. Like Laplanders do with their reindeer. Or Masai with their cattle. It's economical. The captive is like a walking canteen. Children especially might be nourished that way in times of protein shortage. Of course, we stifled all recollections of the blood cow long ago. All we have left to remember it by is, well, is the hickey.

DAN: Oh. The hickey. The innocent hickey of my childhood. Isn't anything sacred with you? Maureen Fitzhugh gave me a huge blue one on my neck— everyone in my junior class was impressed. Now you tell me she was sucking my blood. Great.

FERGUS: It's perfectly natural. And, in its way, loving. As is, for instance, the bondage fetish. Which goes along with it. The participants in a bondage fantasy, engage in a transaction that goes like this. "I, the dominant, will immobilize you with this rope so that you, the submissive, can't escape. So that you are 'made still.' Otherwise I will get all paranoid and I'll have to kill you and eat you right away." The bondage ball gag, by the way, remembers the savory apple stuck in the roast boar's mouth. Sex covers cannibalism. Sexual fantasies, in general, save lives by allowing people to act out dangerous compulsions.

DAN: Wait a minute. Did your Dawn People have rope?

FERGUS: Of course not.

DAN: Then how—it occurs to me to ask—how do you keep this conveniently docile herd of captives from high-tailing it away some dark night.

FERGUS: Let me answer that with a question.

DAN: Yes?

FERGUS: Doesn't the prevalence of foot fetishism on the modern sexual agenda, doesn't it strike you as interesting? It isn't my cup of tea. Nor yours, I suppose. It isn't exactly what I'd call commonplace. "Prevalence" probably is too strong a word. But it hangs in there.

DAN: When I think of feet I think of bunions and toe jelly.

FERGUS: Uh-huh. But, when I meditated on it, I thought, well... Well, there must be some cannibal guilt hidden under this fetish, too. Yes, feet apparently taste good—modern Polynesian cannibals tell us that. But so do hands taste good—and I don't think I've ever heard much talk about hand fetishes. So what gives here? Why do feet have such special meaning?

DAN: Has this become a general question? Are you addressing me?

FERGUS: Well, I'm just taking you through my thought processes. So. So, all at once it hit me. That's how they controlled the captive herd. They bruised or broke the feet. Not casually. They did it as a matter of practice. And the procedure must have become, after a while, must have become quite sophisticated. Degrees of damage might be induced. You want complete immobility, break the feet entirely. A shuffling gait, so the victim can keep up with the tribe? Well, then you break one foot or a couple of toes. When you come to think about it, feet are both essential and supremely vulnerable. The sign of the captive was a broken foot. Hominids with broken feet were eaten. Hominids with healthy feet belonged to the ruling tribal family. So comes our sexual fascination with the foot. By reaction formation the foot, symbol of vulnerability, inspires a complex fetish—the foot is turned into an object of beauty and appetite and fear. Sex covers cannibalism. Again.

DAN: That's why men like women to wear high heels—they become members of the captive herd. Oh. Owww. My damn leg fell asleep. Nnnng. Nnnng. Wow, that's one of life's worst minor pains. Ow. Listen, I can't hack this any longer. Let's get a move on. Huh? I'm turning claustrophobic. And I know, I know, I'm gonna brain myself on one of these pipes.

FERGUS: Yeah, but... I mean, what do you think about it?

DAN: About what?

FERGUS: My theory of sex and cannibalism?

174

DAN: What can I say? I'm not Joseph Campbell. I'm an easy mark. You're a great storyteller—

FERGUS: Oh, how patronizing. I'm telling little fairy stories.

DAN: I don't mean it that way. Damn, the last candle's gone out. Put your flashlight on.

FERGUS: Dan. I need some praise here. I've taken risks to get this far. It isn't fun digging that deep into the Collective Unconscious. It's not a place where you meet friends. The neighborhood stinks.

DAN: Well, that's sorta what I've been saying. You've been under stress. And famished. Don't you think that might—might, I say—might lead to some excesses? You need time to think this over in tranquillity. So do I.

FERGUS: Tranquillity? There's no tranquillity for me. How can I ever be tranquil again?

DAN: Give yourself a holiday. Regular food. Bourbon when you want it. Stop being a desert father for a while.

FERGUS: But this is important. It helps us to see how the world works. Not just on the human level—on the national level, too. Take the Holocaust. There you see the kill-eat instinct rising from the Unconscious of an entire people. Jews, while not literally devoured, were made into soap and lampshades. In fact, the whole of Eastern Europe became a vast digestive system. Railroads were the intestinal tract. Each concentration camp was a stomach, where Jews were stripped and plucked. And then—what?—then baked in ovens. What more do you want? It's pretty clear isn't it?

DAN: All right, all right. Ow. What'd I tell you? I knew I'd hit my head on a pipe. Put the flashlight on, dammit. I don't want—

[*The B side of my second tape ran out just then. Fergus held the flashlight—it shook like a strobe in his hand—while I reloaded. New tape, of course, comes wrapped from the factory in this paint-tight, super-strong cellophane that you (I, anyway) end up gnawing with my teeth. Until that moment Fergus and I had agreed not to notice my tape recorder—though he was well aware of it. To some degree, I imagine, he was performing—how else to explain the remarkable* orderliness *in his arguments? There were passages also that had a kind of memorized, unspontaneous cadence to them: worked out, I guess, sentence by sentence, through his empty disenfranchised days and nights. In any case, it had been an athletic bit of theatre. And he was bushed.*

It took me about fifteen minutes to get Fergus up and around. We were both stiff—he from arthritis, me from a continual and sudden cringing (I didn't want to touch anything down there). Then together we managed to collect and secure his "papers"—an unprepossessing sheaf of newsprint (so I thought) with gnomic sayings written in pencil along the margins. Then we both had to urinate, about which enough said. During this time, Fergus required considerable direction and encouragement, as well as praise. He was, I think, not only tired, but also afraid of having to buck the cold once more. Finally, though, he began to feel hunger again. And I—despite the aroma and decay and feces—I did, too.

The journey out was probably shorter. (In total distance covered, at any rate.) After about ten minutes of spelunking, however, Fergus made a right hand turn that appeared to double back on itself. He could smell food, or so he told me. I smelled general stench—when, that is, I smelled at all. Mostly, I had been breathing through my mouth, which, by then, was dry as kapok and tasted of burned metals. I gave Fergus a hard time: it seemed to me wiser that we get home first. But Fergus, in his passive-aggressive manner, ignored me and began walking faster. What choice did I have? I was blind and clueless without him. So I followed.

Into what was evidently a living room—such, in prototype, as you might have found on the Upper West Side around 1975 or so. Bookshelved walls, African art, a hookah used as a bong, oriental tapestries, and a photo of Lenin. There were two bulbless floor lamps around a coffee table with copies of Esquire *and* Playboy *and the* New York Review of Books *on it. An orange cat, lying curled like a large croissant, slept in the reading chair. It was a monument to the resiliency (or to the bull-headedness) of the middle class in threadbare circumstances.*

Bascum, who lived, apparently, in this catacomb of the bourgeoisie, had been tending a stew. Two Sterno cans flared atop the coffee table. He reminded me of Gene Hackman—wild-haired and balding, nose like a walnut. Bascum had a dressing gown on. It opened, as he stirred the pot, to show a bearish, heavy-breasted torso. Fergus and he evidently knew each other well enough to exchange literate insults. Then, with a reluctance mitigated by pride, Bascum offered us each a small bowl. Fergus scarfed his down. I would have refused, but it became a matter of etiquette. And, to tell the truth, I was ravenous by that time.

Tape 3, side A begins just after the meal.]

BASCUM: It's good, huh, isn't it? Tell me what you think of it, huh?

DAN: Good. Tomato and—

BASCUM: Tomatoes I stole. And onions I, huh, found. Carrots I got for a Steel Sack full of aluminum cans.

FERGUS: I could use some more, just a cup more. And stir from the bottom, where the meat is. You taste the meat, Dan?

DAN: Well, it was chewy.

BASCUM: I, huh, thought it was good. You know what the meat was?

DAN: No.

FERGUS: Human flesh.

DAN: What?

BASCUM: Why do you haveta say that, Gus? It's not true.

FERGUS: But how does he know? You could be some serial killer, marinating a human leg down here.

BASCUM: Ignore him—he's a nut with his cannibalism talk. The meat is chamois cloth, cut up fine. I stole it from a window washer. A whole pile of it, new.

DAN: Chamois cloth?

BASCUM: New. Don't, huh, worry. It was new.

FERGUS: Bascum is famous for his meat improvisations.

BASCUM: Long as it won't kill you. Eat it, I always say. I ate a leather hat last week.

DAN: Chamois cloth?

FERGUS: Leather hats. And still Bascum says he'll never get hungry enough to eat human flesh.

BASCUM: I don't say, "Never." Anything's possible. But I'd rather not.

FERGUS: Yet you gulp down Jesus on Sunday. You perform a cannibal act without the slightest compunction.

BASCUM: Don't let him get started on that. On that subject. Bread and wine, flesh and blood. He'll chew your ear off. And then eat it probably.

DAN: What about the bread and wine?

BASCUM: Here we go again.

FERGUS: You both think I'm crazy. You think I'm obsessing. Well, then, explain why the focal Christian rite—the Eucharist—is cannibalistic. Sanctioned by God, *insisted on* by God. "Take, eat, this is my body. This is my blood—"

DAN: But that's just symbolic.

FERGUS: Oh, is it? I don't think so. I think the sacrifice and the eating are very real. Certainly Jesus's death on the cross was very real. So real we're afraid of it. Still. For twenty centuries we've been trained to act out a euphemized and anti-septic sacrament. Wafers and grape juice. Because Christians are afraid of the

178

crucifixion and the Eucharist. Afraid of seeing through them, into them. On a beautiful Sunday morning, with his children around him, no Christian wants to remember that he's eating human flesh. But he is. A terrible cannibalism—there's no other word for it. Jesus is man. We eat him. That's cannibalism. We inflict a horrible death on Him-Whom-we-love-most. And a horrible desecration of His body. Suppose that wafer you just ate was Jesus's finger joint? His ear, an eyeball, a piece of thigh?

DAN: Stop trying to shock—

FERGUS: Shock? It's the simple truth, that's all. I'm tired of the prettified crucifixion. "This is my body," that's what He said. My *body*. With arms and legs and sweat and blood. Little old ladies with blue hair and false teeth—they eat a dead man's body on Sunday before the altar guild meeting. Talk about serial killers. Innocent children at their first communion suck the blood out of a corpse. I've got to state it in such graphic terms, otherwise we'll never break through to God's meaning. Unless you understand the shocking reality of the sacrifice, you'll never understand the shocking reality of the atonement.

BASCUM: Calm down, Gus.

FERGUS: See, there is yet another profound contradiction at the heart of Christianity. No one wants to talk about it, Dan. Bascum won't accept it. It marks a visceral disagreement, a falling-out between man and God. Simply put: *We don't want to eat Jesus.* And we're furious with God for making us do it. We hate cannibalism. Especially we hate to eat the sinless Son of God. And yet we have to do it. Jesus commanded us to eat His body. We don't—in modern times—cannibalize our worst enemy, let alone our Holy Savior. So—at some central place in our collective psyche—eating the Eucharist has always been a heinous and revolting ordeal. That's why we've dressed it up. That's why we block the thought of Jesus's actual body—skin and hair and mucus. Because we've forgotten our own history. We don't remember our origins.

DAN: Our origins in what?

BASCUM: In cannibalism. That's his point. We're in denial. He says.

DAN: In denial.

FERGUS: We've buried the tribal memories of cannibalism so deep that they now lie in the darkest part of the Unconscious. So what do we have? We have a faith—Christianity—that is totally out of proportion. Jesus dies and is eaten so that my sins can be absolved. What kinda lousy trade-off is that? My sins? Pride, lust, little piddling acts of unlove—for that mess *almighty God* is going to be killed and eaten? Uh-uh. No sir. I know my place. I know that the salvation of my soul is not worth the eating of Jesus Christ. And God has given us free will. I can say, "No thanks," when Jesus offers His body. "Thanks, but no thanks, I'm unworthy, I'll pass this time." Because—I don't know about you—but I'd rather go to hell than perform a cannibal act on God's body. I'm not worth it.

BASCUM: Sit in the armchair.

DAN: As a creation of God you are also a part of God.

FERGUS: Dan, what I'm trying to do, I'm trying to show you the process of my thought. I was starving—Bascum found me—as close to death as you can be. And this is what lodged in my mind, the last thought. That I was pissed off at God because His forgiveness didn't fit the crime. It was too big. God had condemned me to a frightening lifetime of cannibal rites at an altar. For what? Why did I deserve such a gruesome salvation? Why did I *need* it? And then I thought, wait a minute. Cannibalism in the communion service, maybe it's not so gratuitous as it seems. Or out of proportion. Maybe we eat His body and drink His blood in expiation of a specific cannibal act. If not committed by me, then committed by my ancestors, by my blood. Once upon a time.

DAN: And that's what led you to dig beneath your sexuality?

FERGUS: Yes. Because it is all so outrageous otherwise. People of the millennium, people who fly to the moon, still gather on Sunday to act out a cannibal feast. It's either absurd beyond hope or it hides a mysterious and liberating truth. That Jesus was killed and is eaten at the altar to free us from the consequences of a particular cannibalistic incident. A sin—though perhaps committed under extenuating circumstances—a sin that we all share in.

BASCUM: Okay, enough. You've given Dan enough to think about already. Stop it.

FERGUS: I will, I will. After I finish. I need to tell him about my vision. Because it's optimistic, I think. It's the important thing I've got to say.

DAN: How long is this?

FERGUS: Ten minutes, fifteen minutes, then we'll go. Don't pressure me to hurry. My lungs hurt.

DAN: All right. Go on.

FERGUS: Listen. Jesus is the tribal father. The one who sacrifices His body in the time of famine so that His children may live. Goes willingly to death. And we are the children who will forever feel guilt. And anger. It is, after all, not our fault that the body demands constant sustenance. The brain, the soul, the spirit— if they could—they would refuse to kill for food, I think. But that, for some reason, is how God created us. Half beast, half angel. He found the tension to be useful. In time He taught us to forswear human sacrifice—that's the meaning of the Abraham and Isaac story. Rams, not children, are to be killed and eaten. But only through Jesus's sacrifice could God heal our cannibal memories, heal our guilt for cannibal acts that had been committed in the past. That's why Jesus has to die and be eaten.

DAN: And yet, because we don't recognize the cannibal nature of our past, we can't, well, appreciate what God has done for us.

FERGUS: Right. It seems so over-the-top. So peculiarly cruel and brutal. Jesus is taken captive, then put in bondage. Then He is scourged, flagellated, to tenderize His flesh. Then He is bled on the cross. Then, over a long period of time, His body, miraculously preserved, His body is eaten in a continuing rite.

But there is no titillation in this. Remember, as I've been telling you, our sexual sensibility evolved to cover and soften cannibal events. But the cannibalistic sacrifice of Jesus on Golgotha has no sexual story to cover it. Sex doesn't belong in the Jesus narrative. There is no cover. And that's where the churches come in. They can't provide sexual cover, of course, but they can provide *sensuos* cover: the music, the art, the vestments, the ritual, they draw attention away from the eaten Jesus. The churches are a surrogate for our sexuality.

BASCUM: That part maybe I agree with. The, huh, neurotic part. And the priests get a chance to dress in drag on Sunday.

FERGUS: Again, understand—I'm describing my thought processes. This all took place over, say, a month—during which month I was hospitalized for malnutrition. So I'll be the first to grant it, I was a wee bit strange. In this state of mind I had a vision. Call it a dream if it makes you feel more comfortable. Remember, all that time, maybe six weeks, I haven't gone to church. I've taken this Byronic stance of noble detachment. No, I won't eat or drink Jesus because I'm not worthy. I'm not deserving. Anyway. Anyway, I had this vision. I'm kneeling over a dead body, male or female, I'm not sure, the body is lying naked on its stomach. And I'm incredibly hungry. And maybe I feel guilt, but it all seems perfectly natural. I lean down over the corpse and I break it's right shoulder off. To eat it.

DAN: Break it off?

FERGUS: Yes. Break it off. Because, you see—the body was made of bread.

DAN: It wasn't a real body?

FERGUS: No, it was real. It was real. In some mystical way it was real. And, just as surely, in some mystical way it was also made of bread. And I thought, *eureka*, I've found it, I understand transubstantiation. Catholics, among others, believe that the bread and the wine turn into Jesus's real flesh and His real blood during the Mass. At the elevation of the Host, specifically. But they're just half right. Yes, there is transubstantiation, but it occurred once and once only—*at the Last Supper*. Do you get what I'm saying?

DAN: No, spell it out.

FERGUS: When Jesus said, "This is my body, this is my blood," when He said those words, well, all bread and all wine, for all time were (and will be) imbued with Christ's nature and the nature of His body and blood. *All* bread and *all* wine. There is no cannibalization of Jesus at the Mass. Bread and wine, of themselves, are a sufficient sacrificial offering, because they were made *different* at the Last Supper. The inner form of bread and the inner form of wine were changed forever. All the bread and all the wine we eat—in church and out of church—can potentially be part of the ongoing Eucharist. *For those who believe.* This is where faith comes in. For those who don't believe, for them bread is bread and wine is wine. The hidden, sacred nature of the bread and the wine is not available to them. Because they have not assented to its presence.

DAN: So let me get it straight. After all you've put us through, after all that, there is no cannibalism at the altar rail?

FERGUS: No. Since the day after Calvary we've missed the point. Missed the point and, worse, felt great distress and pain, because we have been compelled to eat our Lord on Sunday morning. Truth is: Jesus's body and blood have already and finally changed. Jesus is our daily bread. And our daily bread is Jesus. He is transfigured. And so is bread.

BASCUM: Well, I'll say this, huh—bread looks, how you say, *physical*. Thighs, you know, look like loaves of bread. Crust is skin. You could go on. When bread is soaked in wine it looks like a piece of bloody flesh.

FERGUS: Never mind the looks. Bread satisfies—that's the important thing. Satisfies as much as meat satisfies. Without the killing. It can replace meat—just as sex replaces cannibalism.

BASCUM: Bread allows the hunter-gatherer to settle down. Store food in case of famine.

FERGUS: He is less afraid of being eaten. Instead of staring with cannibal lust at a human thigh, he can stare with hunger at a loaf of bread. And break off the "heel" and eat it.

BASCUM: "Rolls" of flesh.

FERGUS: When I said before that sexual touching—"feeling up" as we say—that such touching is part of a subconscious inspection process—we touch one another to find the best cuts of meat—when I said that, well, I wasn't being precise enough. The sexual touch is closer to kneading. Bread sensuality has replaced flesh sensuality. Who doesn't love to squeeze a loaf of bread, a lump of dough? Who?

BASCUM: I knew a woman, her breasts looked and felt like kaiser rolls. Huh. Exactly.

FERGUS: Remember—at any level—eating is a mysterious business. It goes back to the ancient philosophers, who held, as an axiom, that two objects cannot occupy the same space. Cannot interpenetrate each other. On such sensible thoughts modern science has constructed itself. All this is self-evident. A house can't exist where a bridge exists. A tree can't pass through a wall, without knocking the wall down first. And yet, if a tiger eats you—well, you and the tiger interpenetrate, against all the precepts of ancient physics. It was a most disturbing idea. If I eat you, then you and I come to occupy the same space. The substance of me becomes the substance of you literally. Atoms mix. The ancients didn't know that for sure, though Lucretius and others must have considered it. For most, though, it was a magical idea. Most assumed that, if A ate B, then *both* the substance *and* the essence of B became part of A. You could eat virtue. Eat bravery, eat strength, eat intelligence. But the essence is not transferable. To attain the essence you must have faith. As you must have faith at the altar rail—otherwise you receive only the substance of bread and wine.

BASCUM: I look at all this from a Marxist point of view. Cannibalism is not— not a thing of the past. The working Joe has always, always, been eaten by the capitalist pig. We've had fifty years of a booming market. Why? Because it's been built on the corpses—hundreds of millions of them—corpses of the human beings who died in World War II. Talk about blood sacrifice and cannibalism. Your Dawn Man, if he ever existed, was a *pisher* rookie when it came to cannibalism. You see the homeless lining up outside a blood bank—sucking them dry. If I could just get your mind off heaven and onto politics instead—you might do some good for a change.

DAN: Let's go home now, Fergus. Let's let Mr. Bascum eat his chamois.

BASCUM: Go with him, Fergus. I can't feed you.

FERGUS: Sure. I always intended to. I was just earning my supper. Well? So?

DAN: Well, so what?

FERGUS: Is it good? My Theophysics? Did it have an organic structure? Did it ring a bell with you? In other words: have I been wasting my time? Am I insane? What?

BASCUM: Next time I see a sexy black woman on the street, I'll think of pumpernickel.

FERGUS: I wasn't talking to you. I know already what you think. Dan?

DAN: Well, I don't know. It's interesting, of course—

FERGUS: Interesting? Interesting? I recarve the human psyche, and you call it interesting? Thanks so much for your time. I shouldn't have bothered—

DAN: Wait, wait. Hold on here a minute. I've let you have your say, and I don't care for all this bullying. You want me to give you an answer, then give me time to think about it. You inundate me with ideas and images I'm not familiar with, and you expect me to sign on the dotted line as soon as you finish your song and dance. Remember, for better or worse, I haven't been living night and day with this material.

FERGUS: You don't have to—

DAN: Let me finish. Let someone else speak for once.

BASCUM: Amen.

DAN: You see, you're like someone who's been through medical school—you've trained yourself to cut up cadavers and not be squeamish about it. I haven't, most people haven't. And when you invite us into the morgue, well, we're gonna get a little panicky. We're gonna avert our eyes. Certainly it'll be hard for us to concentrate on your lecture about human anatomy. This is rough stuff for us ordinary mortals. I'm not sure I want to pursue truth—not if the search leads me in that direction. I'm not sure I could live that way. Maybe some of us aren't ready. But, I promise this, if you come home with me, I'll give it a try.

FERGUS: All right. Let me take a leak first, then we'll go.

BASCUM: Use the storeroom behind the steam pipes. Straight down the corridor you came through, then to the left.

FERGUS: Give me my flashlight. You wait here, Dan. I need privacy.

BASCUM: Go straight. No, keep going further. To your left.

DAN: Did I hurt his feelings?

BASCUM: Sure. So-huh. So do I. He's very sensitive. Like, you know, his brain and his body are the same thing. If you don't accept his ideas, you do him physical injury. I mean, I've never seen anyone like Fergus, and we, huh—we tend to looniness down here. He should be dead. The way he's treated his body, he should've died long ago. But his ideas hold him together.

DAN: Well, I'll get him to my place, give him some sensory input.

BASCUM: He's not, huh, coming back.

DAN: What? What do you mean? I can still see his light. It hasn't moved.

BASCUM: It's probably lying on the floor where he left it. He doesn't need the light. That was for, huh, your benefit and he wanted you to have it—but he didn't want you to follow him with it. He needed time to get away.

DAN: Fergus! Fergus! Fergus, answer me!

BASCUM: He did you a favor, believe me. He'd make a lousy roommate. He has horrible seizures. Like a rag doll being shaken by a terrier. Awful, awful. It would've made your life miserable. He's not fit for human companionship, he knows that.

DAN: Fergus! Fergus!

BASCUM: Let it alone.

DAN: But he left me here. How can I find my way out?

BASCUM: Oh, no problem. That door right there, beside the bookshelf, it leads outside.

DAN: Outside? You mean I'm on the surface? I'm not underground?

BASCUM: Go through the door, turn right and up the staircase, you'll be there.

DAN: Where?

BASCUM: Beside the river.

[*I flipped my recorder off then.*

Bascum was correct. I made one turn, ten yards from the door, went up twelve steps and saw the frigid Hudson. I was at the mouth of a monster storm drain. It inhaled cyclonic wind from the river: I was afraid it would suck Fergus's manuscript from my grip. Jersey, in the distance, sulked behind its Palisades. A cruise ship, lit like a bank of votive candles, headed south.]